Series/Number 07-100

MULTIVARIATE TESTS FOR TIME SERIES MODELS

JEFF B. CROMWELL
West Virginia University

MICHAEL J. HANNAN
Edinboro University of Pennsylvania

WALTER C. LABYS
West Virginia University

MICHEL TERRAZA
University of Montpellier I, France

SAGE PUBLICATIONS
International Educational and Professional Publisher
Thousand Oaks   London   New Delhi

For information address:

SAGE Publications, Inc.
2455 Teller Road
Thousand Oaks, California 91320

SAGE Publications Ltd.
6 Bonhill Street
London EC2A 4PU
United Kingdom

SAGE Publications India Pvt. Ltd.
M-32 Market
Greater Kailash I
New Delhi 110 048 India

Printed in the United States of America

Multivariate tests for time series models / Jeff B. Cromwell . . . [et al.].
    p.   cm.—(A Sage university papers series. Quantitative applications in the social sciences; no. 07-100)
    Includes bibliographical references.
    ISBN 0-8039-5440-9 (pbk.)
    1. Time-series analysis. 2. Social sciences—Statistical methods.
    I. Cromwell, Jeff B.   II. Series.
    HA30.3.M85   1994   94-7961
    300′.1′51955—dc20

94 95 96 97 98   10 9 8 7 6 5 4 3 2 1

Sage Production Editor: Astrid Virding

When citing a university paper, please use the proper form. Remember to cite the current Sage University Paper series title and include the paper number. One of the following formats can be adapted (depending on the style manual used):

(1) CROMWELL, J. B., HANNAN, M. J., LABYS, W. C., and TERRAZA, M. (1994) *Multivariate Tests for Time Series Models.* Sage University Paper series on Quantitative Applications in the Social Sciences, 07-100. Thousand Oaks, CA: Sage.

OR

(2) Cromwell, J. B., Hannan, M. J., Labys, W. C., & Terraza, M. (1994). *Multivariate tests for time series models* (Sage University Paper series on Quantitative Applications in the Social Sciences, series no. 07-100). Thousand Oaks, CA: Sage.

CONTENTS

SERIES EDITOR'S INTRODUCTION

In their earlier, companion volume, *Univariate Tests for Time Series Models* (No. 99 of this series), the authors laid the groundwork for the explanation of tests for univariate stochastic (random) time series models. With such analysis, an essential first question is, "Does the stochastic process change over time?" If, for variable X, the answer is "yes," then it is *nonstationary*. A typical example of a nonstationary time series is United States Gross National Product (GNP), which has generally drifted upward since the 1930s (considering its more or less steadily rising mean value over the period). Upon reflection, it is obvious that many social science variables measured across time are nonstationary. Lamentably, uncritical analysis of nonstationary time series can generate spurious results.

Take the hypothetical example of Dr. Brown, a public policy analyst interested in the relationship between GNP (a nonstationary variable) and Federal Government Spending (another nonstationary variable). To estimate the relationship, suppose Dr. Brown employs ordinary least squares, regressing Spending on GNP. If one observes a highly significant slope coefficient for the GNP variable, it may simply be spurious, a product of the nonstationarity in the two series. Before analysis, if these series had been made *stationary* by *differencing* [e.g., $y(t) - y(t-1)$], perhaps faulty inference could have been avoided.

Herein, the authors start out with stationarity testing, remarking that, as compared to univariate applications, multivariate applications are few. They develop the *joint stationarity* test—that of Fountis and Dickey, then go on to discuss transformations to achieve stationarity, featuring differencing. In Chapter 3, they turn to testing for *cointegration*. When two nonstationary time series variables combine to generate a stationary error process in a regression, they are held to be *cointegrated*. If such were found to be the case in the above example of GNP and Federal Spending, then the inference of a significant link between the two might not be spurious after all. The authors describe various cointegration tests, the most straightforward of which utilizes the well-known Durbin-Watson statistic.

Remaining chapters build on these fundamental ideas, lucidly exploring a variety of cutting-edge multivariate time series topics—Granger causality, transfer functions, vector autoregression, to name some leaders. The final chapter gives helpful guidance on computer software. Although these two volumes treat sophisticated material, they do so in a way accessible to interested researchers who have a working knowledge of time series regression. Thus, in reading the Sage papers, they are the logical and important next step after Ostrom (*Time Series Analysis: Regression Techniques*, No. 9, second edition). Upon absorbing these time series tests, the analyst will be prepared for very serious work.

—*Michael S. Lewis-Beck*
Series Editor

MULTIVARIATE TESTS
FOR TIME SERIES MODELS

JEFF B. CROMWELL
West Virginia University

MICHAEL J. HANNAN
Edinboro University of Pennsylvania

WALTER C. LABYS
West Virginia University

MICHEL TERRAZA
University of Montpellier I, France

1. INTRODUCTION

Time series analysis has advanced from univariate modeling based on a single variable to multivariate models that employ the interrelationships between several such variables. Constructing such models requires the performing of tests to determine and to discover the interactions that exist between a given time series variable and one or more other variables. That given variable can be influenced not only by certain exogenous events occurring at particular points in time but also by contemporaneous, lagged, and leading values of a second variable or additional variables. Unfortunately, the task of deciphering possible relationships between two or among a group of variables is a difficult one.

AUTHORS' NOTE: We would like to thank the following individuals for their comments on previous portions of this manuscript: Montague Lord, Veronique Murcia, David Sorenson, Jacqueline Khorassini, Douglas Mitchell, Paul Labys, Chen Lin, Fujimoto Hiroaki, and Yongjie Hu. Our appreciation is also due to graduate students in the Econometrics Seminar at West Virginia University and the Time Series Seminar at the Inter-University Consortium for Political and Social Science Research at the University of Michigan. Assistance was also received from the Regional Research Institute at West Virginia University. We would especially like to thank Michael Lewis-Beck, Clive Granger, Jim Granato, and Henry Heitowit for their advice and encouragement.

1

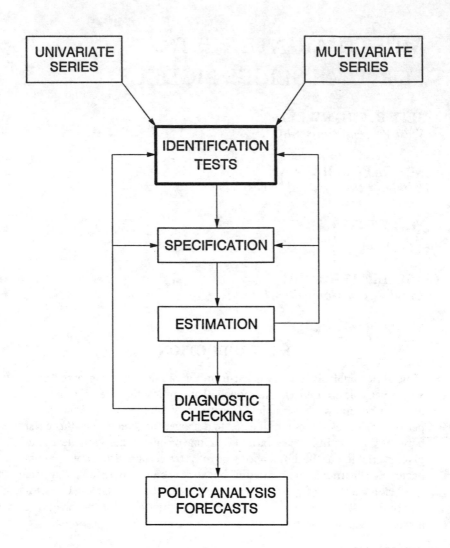

Figure 1.1. Time Series Modeling Approach

In fact, Anderson (1958), Box and Jenkins (1976), Granger and Newbold (1986), Hannan (1970), and Quenouille (1957), among others, assert that the most difficult stage of model building is this first or model identification stage. Figure 1.1 shows the additional stages that include specification, estimation, and diagnostic checking. Historically, only a few time series tests have been available to enable researchers to choose a particular model that might adequately describe the interactions among a set of time series variables. Although a much greater number of such tests is available today, a larger task meets us in deciding which tests, in fact, should be employed.

The purpose of this monograph is to provide practical guidelines for social scientists concerning the nature of these increasingly complex tests and their application in identifying multivariate time series models. Methods for identifying univariate models appear in a preceding monograph by J. Cromwell, W. Labys, and M. Terraza, *Univariate Tests for Time Series Models* (1994). That study will be cited here as UTM.

Relations Between Variables

The notion of a vector time series begins with the concept of a *vector* stochastic or random process, which is defined as an ordered collection of random vectors indexed by time $X(t_1)$, $X(t_2)$, . . . , $X(t_n)$. Time series data that can be employed by social scientists and thus described by such variables tend to be measured in discrete units, that is, daily, monthly, yearly, and so forth. An example of two sample time series or realizations of a vector stochastic process is given in Figure 1.2. The two series shown are: (1) quarterly macropartisanship data on the party identification of voters (MACRO) beginning in January 1953 and extending to December 1988, and (2) the Michigan index for consumer sentiment (MIS) sampled over the same time period. The macropartisanship data have been developed by Stimson (1991) through the appropriate combining of several major voter surveys, while their time series properties have been tested by MacKuen, Erikson, and Stimson (1992).

In order to test for possible interrelationships between these series, several important statistical concepts are first needed.

Joint Stationarity

Assume that one has a stochastic vector of m variables with T observations on each variable, that is, $X(t) = [x_1(t), x_2(t), . . . , x_m(t)]$. This vector is called an *m-dimensional (discrete) vector stochastic process*. This vector stochastic process is characterized by its joint distribution, which for our purposes refers to the first two moments (i.e., mean and variance) of this distribution.

4

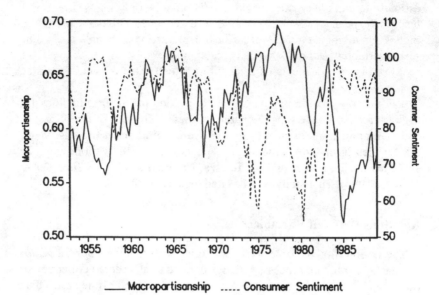

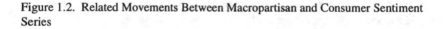

Figure 1.2. Related Movements Between Macropartisan and Consumer Sentiment Series

Recall that in the univariate case, Judge, Griffiths, Hill, Lutkepohl, and Lee (1985) state that if a time series is distributed normally, the first two moments, mean and variance, provide all necessary information regarding the time series. This is also true in the multivariate context. Therefore, one often accepts this assumption and examines the constancy of the mean and variance of the stochastic vector with respect to time.

Similar to a univariate process, a vector stochastic process $X(t)$ is called *jointly wide sense stationary* if the first two moments are finite and constant with respect to time. Using the expectations operator, we can write this condition formally as

$$E[X(t)] = \mu < \infty \qquad \text{for all } t \qquad (1.1)$$

$$E\{[X(t) - \mu][X(t) - \mu]'\} = \Sigma_x < \infty \qquad \text{for all } t \qquad (1.2)$$

Given that the first two conditions are satisfied, one also has

$$E\{[X(t) - \mu][X(t + k) - \mu]'\} = \Gamma_X(k) \qquad \text{for all } t \text{ and } k \qquad (1.3)$$

where $\Gamma_X(k)$ is the covariance and cross-covariance matrix at lag k. It is important for this theoretical condition to hold, as it did in the univariate case discussed in UTM.

Covariance and Correlation

Given that the joint stationarity (in the wide sense) assumption is satisfied, the autocovariance and autocorrelation functions provide information about the individual structure (i.e., nature of the dependence) of each series; however, the use of these concepts with several series requires that we also examine the cross-dependencies that exist among series. These cross-dependencies or cross-correlations can be defined through their respective cross-covariance and cross-correlation functions, as presented below in (1.4). The function $\Gamma_{ij}(k) = \text{cov}[x_i(t), x_j(t + k)]$, where $k = 0, \pm 1, \pm 2, \ldots$ for $i \neq j$, is called the *cross-covariance function* between $x_i(t)$ and $x_j(t)$. The *cross-correlation function* is correspondingly defined by

$$\rho_{ij}(k) = \Gamma_{ij}(k)/[\Gamma_{ii}(0)\Gamma_{jj}(0)]^{\frac{1}{2}} \qquad (1.4)$$

where $\Gamma_{ii}(0)$ and $\Gamma_{jj}(0)$ represent the variances associated with the ith and jth individual series. Therefore, the expression in (1.4) denotes what is referred to as an *autocorrelation matrix* where the diagonal elements are the autocorrelation at lag k for each individual series and the off-diagonal elements represent the cross-correlations between series. In order for us to examine this autocorrelation matrix in the same manner as was suggested by the autocorrelation function, remember that the assumption of joint stationarity in the wide sense *must* again be invoked.

A straightforward application of cross-correlation analysis is the identification of *leading* and *lagging* relations between two time series. For example, consider a relation of the form

$$y(t) = \alpha x(t - k) . \qquad (1.5)$$

The series $x(t)$ "leads" $y(t)$ by k periods for $k > 0$ and "lags" $y(t)$ for $k < 0$. The cross-covariance function is interpreted similarly to the autocovariance function. A peak in value appears on the positive side if $x(t)$ leads $y(t)$, and a peak appears on the negative side if $x(t)$ lags $y(t)$.

TABLE 1.1

A Plot of the Cross-Correlation Function for ΔMACRO and ΔMIS

```
Date: 8-27-1993 / Time: 18:18
SMPL range: 1953.2 - 1988.4
Number of observations: 143
```

COR{ΔMACRO,ΔMIS(-i)}	COR{ΔMACRO,ΔMIS(+i)}	i	lag	lead
| ** | .	| ** | .	0	−0.120	−0.120
| .* | .	| . |**	1	−0.056	0.135
| ** | .	| . | .	2	−0.128	−0.012
| .* | .	| . | .	3	−0.041	−0.003
| . | .	| . |***	4	−0.009	0.212
| .* | .	| . | .	5	−0.102	0.034
| ** | .	| . |*.	6	−0.134	0.048
| . |*.	| .* | .	7	0.048	−0.060
| . |**	| . |*.	8	0.137	0.091
| . | .	| .* | .	9	−0.012	−0.073
| . |**	| .* | .	10	0.131	−0.109
| . | .	| .* | .	11	−0.010	−0.108
| . |*.	| . | .	12	0.079	0.005

| | | SE of Correlations | 0.084 | |

For example, MicroTSP enables one to estimate the cross-correlation for jointly stationary bivariate time series. Table 1.1 provides these estimates for the first differences of the macropartisanship and Michigan index of consumer sentiment variables. The left column plot demonstrates the magnitude of the cross-correlation of using MIS to predict MACRO and the correlations on the right give information regarding which lags enable MACRO to predict MIS. As will be discussed in Chapter 4, the cross-correlation function can also be used in tests of causality.

Clearly, the highest value of the cross-correlation function occurs to the extent that ΔMIS is useful for predicting ΔMACRO at lag four. It is also expected and demonstrated by the plot on the right-hand side that lags of ΔMIS have very little explanatory power with regard to ΔMACRO. One will notice that by varying the lag length k, one obtains different results. Using matrix algebra, one can estimate (1.4) in order to extend this bivariate analysis to the multivariate context.

Time Series Tests and Model Building

The model identification approach adopted here follows a sequential testing procedure, as depicted in Figure 1.3. Although this procedure

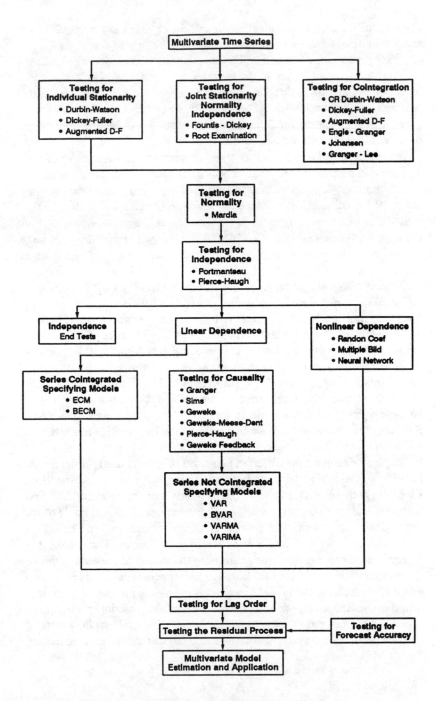

Figure 1.3. Multivariate Test Procedure for Model Identification

appears to be fairly mechanical, a *great* deal of judgment is required in reaching a final model specification. Tests for the first of these sequential steps are presented in Chapter 2. This step begins with stationarity testing, which can be accomplished at the individual or scalar level or at the joint level. Although intimately related to the concept of joint stationarity, tests for cointegration can also be included at this stage; however, they are often performed independently. Other important tests conducted at this stage include normality and independence.

The next sequential step involves tests for cointegration between variables. The more important of these tests appear in Chapter 3, including extensions to multidimensional cointegration and multicointegration. At the next step, the notion of causality and its tests are explained in Chapter 4. Because of the difficulties of interpreting causality, a detailed explanation is provided of the statistical consequences of each of the major tests. These tests can also be used to evaluate independence between the elements in the vector time series.

Chapter 5 provides an explanation of how to employ tests to construct multivariate linear models, a sequential step that follows the discovery of linear dependency. Most important in this respect are model specification, variable selection, and lag determination. Because all three of these tasks are related, the identification of a sequential procedure at this point is arbitrary. Model specification involves selecting from a variety of multivariate relationships, that is, TF, VAR, VARMA, BVAR, ECM, and so forth. In order to fit an appropriate specification to the data, causality tests can be performed in the form of tests for exogenity (or variable selection). Because of the increased interest in nonlinear model specification, Chapter 6 deals with this form of model also.

Chapter 7 examines the different measures or criteria used for determining the lag length in tests of both causality and model specification. Essentially, these tests can be separated into two categories. The first category deals with the typical tests and approaches discussed in UTM for determining lag length. The second category introduces tests based on prediction error as a criterion for selecting lag length. Part of the lag determination process involves examining the underlying assumptions of the vector of residuals from the chosen model specification. This is accomplished by repeating the model identification process just performed; only now one uses the vector of residuals from the selected model specification, instead of the raw data vector itself. Chapter 7 also explains how tests of forecast accuracy can be applied to the multivariate models featured earlier.

2. TESTING FOR JOINT STATIONARITY, NORMALITY, AND INDEPENDENCE

The hypothesis testing framework for the time series properties of joint stationarity, normality, and independence is less developed in the multivariate case, compared to the univariate case. This is especially true when testing for joint stationarity. The only joint stationarity test presented here is the Fountis and Dickey (1989) procedure, which examines the eigenvalues of the coefficient matrix from a vector autoregressive (VAR) specification in order to test for the presence of a unit root. Quite often, researchers do not implement this test but instead rely on examining the scalar properties of the vector, that is, testing the elements of the vector for unit roots (Cromwell & Hannan, 1993). Researchers should also be aware that tests for stationarity are really just tests for non-unit roots. In addition, unit root processes (strictly integrated processes), although referred to as nonstationary, really are an example of one particular nonstationary process and do not constitute the whole class of processes.

Tests for normality and independence are also less developed in the multivariate case compared to the univariate. One available method is the multivariate distribution test developed by Mardia (1970). Another is the graphical method for testing for normality devised by Mage (1982). In the case of independence, the multivariate Portmanteau test has been extended by Hosking (1981), and a test of bivariate independence is due to Pierce and Haugh (1977). In an unpublished manuscript, Baek and Brock (1988) have extended the Brock-Dechert-Scheinkman (1986) (BDS) test presented in UTM to the multivariate case, but no applications are currently available.

Testing for Joint Stationarity

Quite often, the unit root tests discussed in UTM are the only ones that apply to testing for stationarity in the multivariate case. This is due in part to the lack of tests explicitly designed for the multivariate case. Typically, unit root examination in the multivariate case requires eigenvalue and eigenvector examination. This, however, involves first fitting the data to a particular linear multivariate time series model and then examining the eigenvalues from that specification. Note that this one-step process is different from that of discovering underlying properties, transforming, and then specifying a model. As an alternative to this procedure, the Fountis-Dickey test extends the unit root tests discussed in UTM to the multivariate case.

Fountis-Dickey Test

The test proposed by Fountis and Dickey (1989) is a multivariate version of the univariate unit root tests proposed by Dickey and Fuller (1979). It involves examining the eigenvalues of the coefficient matrices from a vector autoregressive (VAR) model.

Test Procedure

Step 1. Estimate a VAR(p) model to the vector $X(t)$.

$$X(t) = A_1 X(t-1) + A_2 X(t-2) + \ldots + A_p X(t-p) + V(t)$$

Step 2. Find the largest eigenvalue, λ_{MAX} based on the following equation:

$$|\lambda^p I - A_1 \lambda^{p-1} - \ldots - A_p| = 0 .$$

Step 3. Form the null hypothesis that $X(t)$ has a unit root.

H_0: $X(t)$ has a unit root
H_A: $X(t)$ does not have a unit root

Step 4. Calculate the test statistic MFD

$$\text{MFD} = T(\lambda_{MAX} - 1)$$

where λ_{MAX} is the largest eigenvalue based on Step 2.

Step 5. For a given significance level, α, obtain the critical value τ from Table 8.5.1 of Fuller (1976). Reject H_0 if

$$|\text{MFD}| > \tau .$$

One of the limitations of the above testing procedure is that of achieving a particular VAR specification in Step 1 (see Chapter 5 for a discussion of VAR models). The power of this test depends on assumptions concerning the residuals made in the VAR specification. It can be expected that the power decreases as one violates the residual assumptions. Of course, this is the basic criticism of the Dickey and Fuller (1979) test. Another criticism is its concern with only one unit root; it is quite possible that in the multivariate context more than one unit root exists. One advantage of this test is that one can perform explicit hypothesis testing, similar to VAR specification using the Fountis-Dickey test. In other model specifications one can only examine the point estimates of the eigenvalues associated with the stationarity conditions of that model specification.

Transformations

Stationarity conditions are violated often enough that we must consider possible data transformations in order to induce stationarity into a vector. This is a necessary step because the failure to incorporate the stationarity assumption into time series analysis does not allow one to identify correctly the appropriate model specification for the vector time series. Most often the assumption made in multivariate time series analysis is that if each component of a vector satisfies a property such as stationarity, then the vector also satisfies this property. As will be discussed later, this is especially true with respect to testing for joint stationarity. As an example, Lutkepohl (1982) states, *"differencing nonstationary univariate component series of a multiple time series to induce stationarity prior to building an AR model for the multivariate generation process is in general inadequate"* (p. 238). Therefore, one must exercise caution with respect to performing transformations on just the scalar components to induce joint stationarity in the vector.

If a unit root is expected to exist in the vector, removal of the unit root can be accomplished by using the methodology due to Fountis and Dickey (1989). The authors demonstrate that their method is the vector analog to differencing in the univariate case. However, this interpretation applies only to their method of testing for stationarity and can only be performed in that context.

Another transformation illustrated in UTM to render the second moment constant was the logarithmic transformation. Because the log transformation is a member of the Box-Cox family of power transformations, one can extend the univariate Box-Cox transformations to the multivariate context. Andrews, Gnanadesikan, and Warner (1971) provide the following multivariate test procedure for determining the appropriate power transformation for the vector.

Test Procedure

Step 1. Choose lambda $\lambda = \lambda^*$, which maximizes Lmax(λ).

$$\text{Lmax}(\lambda) = -(\tfrac{1}{2})T \log |\Sigma| + \sum_{j=1}^{m} (\lambda_j - 1) \sum_{i=1}^{T} \log x_{ij}$$

and

$$\Sigma_{X(\lambda)} = T^{-1} \sum_{i=1}^{T} [X_i(\lambda) - \mu(\lambda)] [X_i(\lambda) - \mu(\lambda)]'$$

and

$$\lambda = (\lambda_1, \ldots, \lambda_m)$$

Step 2. Construct the null hypothesis according to

$H_0: \lambda^* = \lambda_0$
$H_A: \lambda^* \neq \lambda_0$

Step 3. Form the likelihood test statistic

$$\text{LK} = 2[\text{Lmax}(\lambda^*) - \text{Lmax}(\lambda_0)].$$

Step 4. For a given significance level, α, obtain the critical value τ from a chi-square distribution with m degrees of freedom and reject H_0 if

$$\text{LK} > \tau .$$

Typically, transformations in the multivariate context are performed in an arbitrary fashion due to reliance upon a visual inspection of the scalar components of the vector as a testing rationale. One should also note that this type of transformation relies on the assumption that for the true lambda, the series is normally distributed.

Testing for Normality

There are three main reasons why it is important to know if a stationary vector is jointly normally distributed. The first is that when joint stationarity and multivariate normality coincide as in the univariate case, then a linear specification exists for the vector time series. The second reason is that under normality, model estimation by least squares and maximum likelihood methods are equally efficient. The last reason is that knowing the nature of the distribution helps in determining the statistical properties of the tests employed. For example, the distributional properties of most test statistics usually rely on the assumption that the data or the residual process are normally distributed. Although many complex tests for multivariate normality exist, only one is presented here. For the specification and properties of other multivariate normality tests, the reader is referred to Seber (1984).

Skewness and Kurtosis Test

Mardia (1970) has developed multivariate extensions to the univariate measures of skewness and kurtosis presented in UTM. These can be computed by the following formulas

$$b_{1,m} = T^{-2} \sum_i [(X_i - \mu)' \Sigma^{-1}(X_i - \mu)]^3 \quad \text{Skewness} \qquad (2.1)$$

$$b_{2,m} = T^{-1} \sum_i [(X_i - \mu)' \Sigma^{-1}(X_i - \mu)]^2 \quad \text{Kurtosis} \qquad (2.2)$$

where μ is the mean vector of $X(t)$ and $i = 1, \ldots, T$. In the case when the vector $X(t)$ is distributed multivariate normally, the following expectation equalities hold:

$$E[b_{1,m}] = 0$$

$$E[b_{s,m}] = m(m + 2)$$

In order to test the null hypothesis of multivariate normality, Mardia (1970) proposes testing each moment individually. The following test procedure outlines this methodology.

Test Procedure

Step 1. Estimate the skewness and kurtosis coefficients

$$b_{1,m} = T^{-2} \sum_i [(X_i - \mu)' \Sigma^{-1}(X_i - \mu)]^3 \quad \text{Skewness}$$

$$b_{2,m} = T^{-1} \sum_i [(X_i - \mu)' \Sigma^{-1}(X_i - \mu)]^2 \quad \text{Kurtosis}$$

where μ is the mean vector of X.

Step 2. Form the null hypothesis for each measure.

H_0: $X(t)$ is distributed multivariately normally, $N(\mu, \Sigma)$
H_A: $X(t)$ is not distributed normally

Step 3. Calculate the test statistics, A and B.

$$A = 6^{-1}Tb_{1,m} \qquad \text{Skewness}$$

$$B = b_{2,m} - m(m + 2)/[8m(m + 2)/T]^{\frac{1}{2}} \quad \text{Kurtosis}$$

Step 4. For a given significance level, α, choose the critical value τ from a chi-square distribution with f degrees of freedom where $f = 6^{-1}m(m + 1)(m + 2)$ to test the skewness and choose the critical value z from the standard normal distribution to test the kurtosis.

Step 5. Reject H_0 if

$$A > \tau \qquad \text{Skewness}$$

$$|B| > |z| \qquad \text{Kurtosis}$$

Mardia (1970) states that A and B give conservative critical values for $m > 2$ and $T > 50$.

Testing for Independence

In the multivariate context, testing for independence can be divided in two categories. Category 1 refers to independence in each element of the vector $X(t)$. Category 2 refers to independence among the variables in $X(t)$. In reference to the independence of Category 1, we can utilize the methods of UTM for testing the null hypothesis of independence, that is, Box-Pierce, BDS, Runs, Turning Point, and so forth. Testing for Category 2 type of independence (which is related to the causality testing procedure of Chapter 4) requires examining the correlation structure among series. This can be accomplished in a bivariate fashion as in Pierce and Haugh (1977) or in a multivariate fashion as in the Portmanteau test of Hosking (1981). Clearly, examining Category 2 type independence in the bivariate case is problematic, because it ignores the cross-covariances of the other variables. Of course, if these cross-covariances are negligible then one can ignore them, which is often the case in empirical work.

Portmanteau Test

Chitturi (1974) and Hosking (1981) developed and refined a multivariate test of independence based on the univariate version of the Portmanteau test. In order to test the null hypothesis of independence the following test statistic is proposed

$$Q = T \sum_{i=1}^{k} \text{tr}\,(\Sigma_i' \Sigma_0^{-1} \Sigma_i \Sigma_0^{-1}) \qquad (2.3)$$

where T is the sample size, k is the number of lags, tr is the trace operator, and Σ_i is the ith covariance matrix of the variables in the jointly, stationary vector $X(t)$.

Test Procedure

Step 1. Form the null hypothesis of independence for the vector $X(t)$.

H_0: $X(t)$ is independent
H_A: $X(t)$ is not independent

Step 2. For a given number of lags, k, calculate the test statistic Q

$$Q = T \sum_{i=1}^{k} \text{tr}\,(\Sigma_i' \Sigma_0^{-1} \Sigma_i \Sigma_0^{-1})$$

where T is the sample size, k is the number of lags and Σ_i is the ith covariance matrix of the variables in the vector X.

Step 3. For a given significance level, α, obtain the critical value τ from the chi-square distribution with $m^2 K$ degrees of freedom. Reject H_0 if

$$Q > \tau.$$

Pierce-Haugh Test

The Pierce-Haugh Test has generally been addressed as a test of independence. The reader should be cautioned, however, that this test primarily examines the correlation or noncorrelation of series. Only in the case where one can assume normality for the series can the test be applied to independence testing. To apply the test, define the cross-correlation between a pair of series $x(t)$ and $y(t)$ as follows:

$$\rho_{uv}(k) = E[u(t-k)v(t)]/\{E[u^2(t)]E[v^2(t)]\}^{\frac{1}{2}} \tag{2.4}$$

where $u(t)$ and $v(t)$ are white noise processes of $x(t)$ and $y(t)$, respectively, and k is the number of cross-correlations tested. In practice, we replace (2.4) with the sample cross-correlation function

$$r_{uv} = \sum u(t-k)v(t)/[\sum u^2(t) \sum v^2(t)]^{\frac{1}{2}} \tag{2.5}$$

where all terms are defined as above. Haugh (1976) forms this sample cross-correlation into the following statistic,

$$U = T \sum_{k=-M_1}^{M_2} r_{uv}^2(k) \tag{2.6}$$

where T is the number of observations and k is the lag length chosen for the test. Under the null hypothesis that $x(t)$ and $y(t)$ are independent, one estimates (2.6) for $k = M_1$ to M_2. The null hypothesis is rejected if U is greater than the selected critical value from a chi-square distribution with $M_2 + M_1 + 1$ degrees of freedom.

Test Procedure

Step 1. Specify the hypotheses to be tested.

H_0: $x(t)$ and $y(t)$ are independent
H_A: $x(t)$ and $y(t)$ are dependent

Step 2. Filter the series to be white noise. This can be done by obtaining the residuals for the series regressed on lags of itself.

Step 3. Calculate the cross-correlations between the resulting residuals using Equation 2.5.

Step 4. Calculate the test statistic, U, using Equation 2.6 for the chosen lag length k.

Step 5. Accept the alternative hypothesis of causality when the test statistic U is greater than $\chi^2(M_2 + M_1 + 1)$.

As previously stated, testing for independence between variables is intimately related to testing for causality. Consult Chapter 4 for a detailed treatment of this topic.

3. TESTING FOR COINTEGRATION

The concept of cointegration, as developed by Granger and others, examines the presence or absence of an equilibrium relationship between two variables over time (e.g., Engle & Granger, 1987; Granger, 1986). An understanding of cointegration is necessary in order to invoke and to explain the structure of the joint stationarity assumption, as well as to facilitate the development of the error correction model. In many areas, theory offers insights as to why two or more time series may move together over time. For example, economic theory can be used to explain why income and consumption or income and savings may move together over time.

In general, two time series variables can be considered cointegrated if they have the same order of integration and the error process from the regression performed on the untransformed variables (i.e., variables in levels) is stationary. A long-run equilibrium relationship can be said to exist between the two variables, while short-run deviations between them are stationary. A detailed discussion of the cointegrating relationship can be found, for example, in studies such as Bannerjee, Dolado, Galbraith, and Henry (1993), Engle and Granger (1991), and Fomby and Rhodes (1990).

More technically, we can state that a purely nondeterministic univariate time series $x(t)$ is said to be integrated of order d, if the dth difference of $x(t)$ is stationary, denoted by $x(t) \rightarrow \mathrm{I}(d)$. For example, if $x(t)$ is integrated of order one, denoted by $\mathrm{I}(1)$, then the difference transformation, $x(t) - x(t-1)$, also equal to $\Delta x(t)$, will be $\mathrm{I}(0)$. That is, $\Delta x(t)$ is now a stationary time series. We can now generalize to a pair of time series, $x(t)$ and $y(t)$. If both series are $\mathrm{I}(d)$, Engle and Granger (1987) state that any linear combination of $x(t)$ and $y(t)$ will also be $\mathrm{I}(d)$. For cointegration to occur between $x(t)$ and $y(t)$, a constant α must exist such that

$$x(t) - \alpha y(t) = e(t) \tag{3.1}$$

where $e(t)$ is I($d - b = 0$), with $b > 0$ and $d \geq 0$. In this general case, $x(t)$ and $y(t)$ are cointegrated of order d,b, written as CI(d,b), where d refers to the order of integration, and $b > 0$ must exist in order to make the error process of (3.1) stationary, that is, integrated of order zero, I = 0. For example, let $x(t) \rightarrow$ I(1) and $y(t) \rightarrow$ I(1). Upon the condition that α exists, $x(t)$ and $y(t)$ are cointegrated, CI(1,1). This concept can be extended to the case where $X(t)$ is a vector time series, thus making α a cointegrating vector. In this case (3.1) includes all elements in the vector time series in the single regression equation.

The variable $e(t)$ provides further information that can be used in model building. This information is related to the extent that the system $X(t) = [x(t), y(t)]$ is out of equilibrium, and therefore is called the "equilibrium error." For example, if $x(t)$ and $y(t)$ are both I(1) and the equilibrium error is I(0), then $e(t)$ will rarely be different from zero. This requires that $e(t)$ has a zero mean and that $x(t)$ and $y(t)$ have a number of zero crossings, thus making a state of equilibrium for the system probable, that is, cointegration between $x(t)$ and $y(t)$. If, however, $e(t)$ is I(1), then the number of zero crossings will be small and the concept of equilibrium will be less probable and have no practical implications for model building, that is, no cointegration between $x(t)$ and $y(t)$.

For a series to be integrated of order one, I(1), the series must contain a *unit root* or can be described as a random walk. (This issue is discussed in detail in UTM, chap. 2.) Such a series is nonstationary and standard statistical inference on levels in any regression model containing such series breaks down. In general, spurious results can occur in regressing one random walk series on another. In these cases one can difference the random walk series before using them in a regression. Due to a loss of information (i.e., low frequency components) from differencing, however, such transformations may not always be desirable. If the series in question are cointegrated, then a linear combination of the series *will be* stationary so that regression in levels will be possible. Alternatively, if the series are random walks but not cointegrated, spurious results are possible if the regression is performed in levels, thus necessitating differencing.

The problem of testing for cointegration can be thought of as testing for the presence of unit roots in an *estimated* time series. A number of tests have been proposed for determining whether a pair, or in general, a vector of integrated time series are cointegrated. Below, we will present the steps involved in the more popular tests and illustrate their application with the macropartisanship and consumer sentiment data. For all of the tests that follow, it is first required that all univariate time series be integrated of order one, I(1). Therefore, the unit root tests discussed in UTM can be employed again here. Once a collection of variables integrated of order one are obtained, we can proceed with the multivariate tests developed in this section.

Having identified the I(1) series, the next step in testing for cointegration is to perform the cointegrating regression, as defined in (3.1). In the bivariate case, this involves estimating the following equation in levels

$$x(t) = a + \beta y(t) + e(t) . \tag{3.2}$$

Note that the cointegrating regression can have as many as k variables, since the only data required for the cointegration tests obtained are those based on the residuals, $e(t)$. This is known as multidimensional cointegration.

For the examples that follow we will consider the case of cointegration between the two series shown in Figure 1.2: Macropartisanship (MACRO) and consumer sentiment (MIS). Visual evidence suggests no strong long-run equilibrium relationship between the two series, that is, no cointegration.

Cointegrating Regression
Durbin-Watson (CRDW) Test

The most simple test method involves the application of the Durbin-Watson (DW) test statistic to the cointegrating regression, Equation 3.2. The Durbin-Watson statistic (DW) is used to determine if the residuals from (3.2) appear to be stationary. (Remember that the null hypothesis stipulates that the variables are not cointegrated.) The null hypothesis will be accepted if the DW value is zero. Alternatively, the null would be rejected in the case that the DW value is large, indicating the existence of cointegration. In addition to the bivariate relationship presented in (3.2), Engle and Yoo (1987) have developed critical values for the cases when up to five variables are included in the equation. Engle and Granger (1987) point out that most economic data are integrated of order one, I(1), and are not an independent stationary process. One could not in practice know, however, what critical value to use. Nonetheless, the CRDW test can be used to provide a first or preliminary judgment as to the presence of cointegration.

Test Procedure

Step 1. Specify the hypotheses to be tested.

H$_0$: DW = 0 (cointegration does not exist)
H$_A$: DW ≠ 0 (cointegration does exist)

Step 2. Estimate the cointegrating regression between the series, that is, Equation 3.2.

Step 3. Estimate the Durbin-Watson statistic (DW) for the cointegrating regression.

Step 4. Compare the DW statistic to the critical values in Engle and Granger (1987) or in Engle and Yoo (1987) for the cases where three to five series are included in Equation 3.2 (see also Appendix Tables A.1 and A.2). If DW > critical value, accept the alternative hypothesis of cointegration.

Example

Step 1. The hypotheses to be tested are:

H$_0$: DW = 0 (cointegration does not exist)
H$_A$: DW ≠ 0 (cointegration does exist)

Step 2. The cointegrating regression is estimated with the following results:

$$MACRO(t) = 0.7332285 - 0.0013006 \, MIS(t) + e(t)$$
$$t = 1953.1 - 1988.4 \, .$$

Step 3. The resulting DW statistic from the above equation is 0.213815.

Step 4. The critical values for the test from Engle and Granger (1987) are: (1%) .0511, (5%) .0386, (10%) 0.322. Because the calculated DW statistic is less than all of the above critical values, we accept the null hypothesis that cointegration does not exist between the two series.

Dickey-Fuller (DF) Test

The DF test follows the same methodology as was developed in UTM. Effectively, the test examines whether the series has a unit root, where differencing helps to remove the root. The test equation is

$$\Delta x(t) = \alpha_1 x(t-1) + e(t) \tag{3.3}$$

where $e(t)$ is an independent and stationary process. In terms of cointegration testing, the only difference is that the variable $x(t)$ is replaced with the residuals $e(t)$ from the cointegrating regression (3.2). The null hypothesis remains that the series represented in (3.2) are not cointegrated. Critical values for the DF test are in Appendix Table A.1 and in MacKinnon (1990).

Test Procedure

Step 1. Estimate the cointegrating Equation 3.2 between the two variables.

Step 2. Test the null hypothesis that $e(t)$ (from the cointegrating regression) is a random walk in one of three ways, depending on the choice of an intercept and/or trend term.

   (i) $\Delta e(t) = \alpha_1 e(t-1) + u(t)$
  (ii) $\Delta e(t) = \alpha_0 + \alpha_1 e(t-1) + u(t)$
 (iii) $\Delta e(t) = \alpha_0 + \alpha_1 e(t-1) + \beta T + u(t)$

The null hypothesis for each is that cointegration does not exist.

   (i) H_0: $e(t)$ is I(1)
  (ii) H_0: $e(t)$ is I(1) + drift
 (iii) H_0: $e(t)$ is I(1) + drift + stochastic trend

Step 3. For each case i, calculate the test statistic

$$t_i(\alpha_1) = [(\alpha_1 - 0)/\text{SE}(\alpha_1)]$$

where $\text{SE}(\alpha_1)$ is the standard error of α_1. Note that these are simply the t statistics associated with each α_1.

Step 4. Choose the significance level for the test and compare the test statistic to the critical values for each *i* from Appendix Table A.1 or MacKinnon (1990). If $|t(\alpha_1)| > t_c$, we accept the alternative hypothesis of cointegration.

Example

Step 1. The cointegrating equation is estimated between MACRO and MIS with the following results:

$$MACRO(t) = 0.7332285 - 0.0013006 \, MIS(t) + e(t)$$
$$t = 1953.1 - 1988.4 \, .$$

Step 2. The DF test equations are estimated using the residuals from the above equation with the following results:

(i) $\Delta e(t) = -0.1053511 \, e(t-1) + u(t)$
(ii) $\Delta e(t) = -8.093\text{E}^{-05} - 0.01053292 \, e(t-1) + u(t)$
(iii) $\Delta e(t) = 0.0020198 - 0.1088308 e(t-1) - 2.856\text{E}^{-05}T + u(t)$

For all equations $t = 1953.3 - 1988.4$.

Step 3. The *t* statistics on α_1 associated with each above test are found to be:

(i) $t(\alpha_1) = -2.7663872$
(ii) $t(\alpha_1) = -2.7558708$
(iii) $t(\alpha_1) = -2.8257021$

Step 4. The MacKinnon critical values for each case are as follows from MicroTSP:

	1%	5%	10%
(i)	−2.5801	−1.9421	−1.6169
(ii)	−3.4773	−2.8818	−2.5774
(iii)	−4.0250	−3.4419	−3.1453

One could also obtain approximate values from Table A.1 in the Appendix.

The results for cointegration are somewhat mixed. In cases (i) and (ii), the *t* statistics are significant at the 5% and 10% level, respectively. In case (iii), we accept the null hypothesis of no cointegration. It should be noted that neither the intercept nor the trend terms were significant in Equations (ii) and (iii), possibly lending more support to the results for test (i), that is, acceptance of the alternative hypothesis of cointegration.

Augmented Dickey-Fuller (ADF) Test

The ADF test can be employed in situations where the assumption that $e(t)$ in Equation 3.3 is an independent and stationary process may *not* be realized, that is, due to the presence of serial correlation. To accommodate this condition, the DF test is augmented with additional lags of the dependent variable as follows:

$$\Delta x(t) = \alpha_1 x(t-1) + \sum_j \beta_j \Delta x(t-j) + e(t) \tag{3.4}$$

where $j = 1, 2, \ldots, p$, and p is the number of lags chosen for the dependent variable, $\Delta x(t)$. Of course, as in the case of the DF test, when using this method to test for cointegration, we replace $x(t)$ with the residuals from the cointegrating regression (3.2). The null hypothesis remains the same—that the series in Equation 3.2 are not cointegrated.

Test Procedure

Step 1. Estimate the cointegrating Equation 3.2 between the two variables.

Step 2. Test the null hypothesis that $e(t)$ (from the cointegrating regression) is a random walk in one of three ways, depending on the choice of an intercept and/or trend term. Lag order, p, is generally chosen based on a model order test (see Chapter 7).

(i) $\Delta e(t) = \alpha_1 e(t-1) + \sum_j \beta_j \Delta e(t-j) + u(t)$
(ii) $\Delta e(t) = \alpha_0 + \alpha_1 e(t-1) + \sum_j \beta_j \Delta e(t-j) + u(t)$
(iii) $\Delta e(t) = \alpha_0 + \alpha_1 e(t-1) + \sum_j \beta_j \Delta e(t-j) + \delta T + u(t)$

The null hypothesis for each is that cointegration does not exist:

(i) H_0: $e(t)$ is I(1)
(ii) H_0: $e(t)$ is I(1) + drift
(iii) H_0: $e(t)$ is I(1) + drift + stochastic trend

Step 3. For each case i and the chosen lag order p, calculate the test statistic

$$t_i(\alpha_1, p) = [(\alpha_1 - 0)/SE(\alpha_1)]$$

where $SE(\alpha_1)$ is the standard error of α_1 .

Step 4. Choose the significance level for the test and compare the test statistic to the critical values for each i and p from Fuller (1976) or MacKinnon (1990). If $|t(\alpha_1)| > |t_c|$, we accept the alternative hypothesis of cointegration.

Example

Step 1. The cointegrating equation is estimated between MACRO and MIS with the following results:

$$MACRO(t) = 0.7332285 - 0.0013006MIS(t) + e(t)$$
$$t = 1953.1 - 1988.4 .$$

Step 2. The ADF test equations are estimated using the residuals from the above equation. For expository purposes a lag order of 2 (i.e., $p = 2$) will be used for the test equations.

(i) $\Delta e(t) = -0.0896321e(t-1) - 0.0779134\Delta e(t-1)$
$\qquad - 0.1182185\Delta e(t-2) + u(t)$

(ii) $\Delta e(t) = 9.723E^{-05} - 0.0896789e(t-1) - 0.0778315\Delta e(t-1)$
$\qquad - 0.1181991\Delta e(t-2) + u(t)$

(iii) $\Delta e(t) = 0.0029730 - 0.0945004e(t-1) - 0.0795303\Delta e(t-1)$
$\qquad - 0.1186406\Delta e(t-2) - 3.883E^{-05}T + u(t)$

For all equations $t = 1953.4 - 1988.4$.

Step 3. The t statistics associated with each of the above equations follow:

(i) $t(\alpha_1) = -2.2466950$

(ii) $t(\alpha_1) = -2.2394119$

(iii) $t(\alpha_1) = -2.3472106$

Step 4. The MacKinnon critical values for each case are as follows (from MicroTSP):

	1%	5%	10%
(i)	−2.5802	−1.9421	−1.6169
(ii)	−3.4776	−2.8819	−2.5775
(iii)	−4.0254	−3.4421	−3.1454

The results for cointegration are somewhat mixed. Under case (i), the alternative hypothesis is accepted at the 5% significance level, indicating cointegration. Cases (ii) and (iii), however, indicate acceptance of the null hypothesis at each level of significance, indicating no cointegration between the series. It should be noted, however, that in these latter two cases, neither the intercept nor the trend were significant.

Engle-Granger Tests

The Engle-Granger tests include two variations of a vector autoregressive (VAR) model: a restricted and an unrestricted model test (see Chapter 5 for a discussion of VAR models).

The *restricted VAR* test specifies the following two equation VAR(1) model

$$\Delta y(t) = \beta_1 e(t-1) + v_1(t)$$

$$\Delta x(t) = \beta_2 e(t-1) + \gamma \Delta y(t) + v_2(t)$$

(3.5)

where $v_1(t)$ and $v_2(t)$ are considered white noise processes and $e(t)$ are the residuals from Equation 3.2. To perform the test, one estimates (3.2) and (3.5) and calculates the test statistic

$$H_1 = t^2(\beta_1) + t^2(\beta_2)$$

(3.6)

where $t(\beta_1)$ and $t(\beta_2)$ are the t statistics for β_1 and β_2, respectively, from Equation 3.5. As with the earlier tests, the null hypothesis is that cointegration does not exist; critical values for the test can be found in Engle and Granger (1987) and in Appendix Table A.2. As an extension of the above test, an augmented restricted VAR test can be employed in the case where one includes up to p lags of the dependent variable in each equation of

(3.5). The test statistic remains that of Equation 3.6 and the null hypothesis is also the same.

The *unrestricted VAR* test is similar and specifies the following two equation VAR(1) model

$$\Delta y(t) = \beta_1 y(t-1) + \beta_2 x(t-1) + c_1 + v_1(t)$$

$$\Delta x(t) = \beta_3 y(t-1) + \beta_4 x(t-1) + \gamma \Delta y(t) + c_2 + v_2(t)$$

(3.7)

where c_1 and c_2 are constants and $v_1(t)$ and $v_2(t)$ are white noise processes. Under the null hypothesis of no cointegration, the test statistic is defined as

$$H_2 = 2(F_1 + F_2)$$

(3.8)

where F_1 and F_2 are the F statistics for the first and second equations in (3.7), respectively. Alternatively, one can alter (3.7) similarly to that of the restricted VAR case. The augmented unrestricted VAR is the same as (3.7), except that p lags of the dependent variable are again included in each equation. The test statistic is the same as in (3.8) and the critical values for both of these tests are provided in Engle and Granger (1987).

The critical values for the restricted VAR, augmented restricted VAR, unrestricted VAR, and the augmented unrestricted VAR depend on the assumption that the true model is VAR(1) with I(1) variables. If the true model is not first order, then these tests should be discarded in favor of CRDW, DF, and ADF tests. The simulation results of Engle and Granger (1987) and Engle and Yoo (1987) indicate that the DF and ADF tests are quite powerful relative to the other tests.

Test Procedure

Step 1. Specify the hypotheses to be tested:

Restricted VAR Test

H_0: $H_1 = 0$ (cointegration does not exist)
H_A: $H_1 \neq 0$ (cointegration does exist)

Unrestricted VAR Test

H_0: $H_2 = 0$ (cointegration does not exist)
H_A: $H_2 \neq 0$ (cointegration does exist)

Step 2. Estimate the cointegrating regression (3.2) and retain the residuals (if using the Restricted VAR test).

Step 3. Estimate the relevant VAR test equations.

Restricted VAR Test
Equation 3.5

Unrestricted VAR Test
Equation 3.7

Step 4. Calculate the relevant test statistic.

Restricted VAR Test
H_1 in Equation 3.6

Unrestricted VAR Test
H_2 in Equation 3.8

Step 5. Compare the test statistic from Step 4 to the critical values in Engle and Granger (1987), as provided in Appendix Table A.2. We accept the alternative hypothesis of cointegration if the test statistic is greater than the critical values.

Example 1. Restricted VAR Model

Step 1. The hypotheses to be tested are:

H_0: $H_1 = 0$
H_A: $H_1 \neq 0$

Step 2. The cointegrating regression between MACRO and MIS is estimated with the following results:

$$MACRO(t) = 0.7332285 - 0.0013006 \, MIS(t) + e(t)$$
$$t = 1953.1 - 1988.4 .$$

Step 3. The restricted VAR system is estimated (Equation 3.5) with the following results:

$$\Delta\text{MIS}(t) = 3.8823055 \; e(t-1) + v_1(t)$$

$$\Delta\text{MACRO}(t) = -0.1083480e(t-1) - 0.0004358 \; \Delta\text{MIS}(t) + v_2(t) \; .$$

Both equations are estimated for $t = 1953.2 - 1988.4$.

Step 4. The H_1 test statistic is calculated as:

$$H_1 = (0.3948833)^2 + (-2.9194448)^2 = 8.679 \; .$$

Step 5. The critical values from Engle and Granger (1987) are: (1%) 18.3, (5%) 13.6, and (10%) 11.0. Because H_1 is less than all of the critical values, we accept the null hypothesis that cointegration does not exist between the two series.

The reader is reminded that an augmented restricted VAR could also have been estimated by including lags of the dependent variables in each of the equations in Step 3. As a confirmation, such a model was estimated using one lag of the dependent variable with the same conclusions reached as above.

Example 2. Unrestricted VAR Model

Step 1. The hypotheses to be tested are:

H_0: $H_2 = 0$
H_A: $H_2 \neq 0$

Step 2. Recall that the cointegrating regression is not needed for this test.

Step 3. The unrestricted VAR system is estimated following Equation 3.7 with the following results:

$$\Delta\text{MIS}(t) = 3.8312892 - 0.0725282 \; \text{MIS}(t-1) + 3.9709492$$

$$\text{DEMO}(t-1) + v_1(t)$$

$$\Delta\text{MACRO}(t) = 0.0894484 - 0.0002607 \; \text{MIS}(t-1) - 0.1079527$$

$$\text{DEMO}(t-1) - 0.0004954 \; \Delta\text{MIS}(t) + v_2(t)$$

Both equations are estimated for $t = 1953.2 - 1988.4$.

Step 4. The H_2 test statistic is calculated as:

$$H_2 = 2(2.888666 + 3.828655) = 13.435 .$$

Step 5. The critical values from Engle and Granger (1987) and Appendix Table A.2 are: (1%) 23.4, (5%) 18.6, and (10%) 16.0. In all cases, H_2 is less than the critical values indicating acceptance of the null hypothesis, that is, no cointegration. Again, an augmented version of this test is also possible; a one-lag version was estimated with the same conclusions reached as above.

Johansen Test

Testing for cointegration in the multivariate case as opposed to the bivariate case poses two additional problems. The first problem is that one has to decide how to "normalize" the cointegrating relationship. In other words, which variable is relevant to express as a linear combination among the other variables. The second problem is that more than one cointegrating relationship may exist. Engle and Yoo (1987) circumvent the first problem by reporting that only small differences in their results were caused by different normalizations. Their opinion is that normalization is only a problem when no "natural" normalization exists. Therefore, Engle and Yoo (1987) perform the multivariate cointegration test in the same manner as in the bivariate case, except that the critical values for the Dickey-Fuller tests are obtained through Monte Carlo simulations. The latter, which are reproduced in Appendix Table A.3, are based on a maximum of five variables in the cointegrating regression.

As an alternative to the approach of Engle and Yoo (1987), Johansen (1988) developed a procedure based on maximum likelihood techniques that addresses both problems.

Test Procedure

Step 1. Regress $\Delta X(t)$ on $\Delta X(t-1), \ldots, X(t-k+1)$ and $X(t-k)$ on $\Delta X(t-1), \ldots, X(t-k+1)$. Denote the residuals by $R_0(t)$, $R_k(t)$ and the moment matrices by S_{00}, S_{kk}, and S_{k0} where $S_{ij} = T^{-1} \sum_t R_i(t) R_j(t)'$ with i, $j \in \{0,1\}$.

Step 2. Solve the equation

$$|\lambda S_{kk} - S_{k0} S_{00}^{-1} S_{0k}| = 0 .$$

Let E be the matrix of eigenvalues. Then E is normalized by $E' S_{kk} E = I$, where I is the identity matrix.

Step 3. Set the null hypothesis.

H_0: There is at most r cointegrating vectors
H_A: There is at most $r - 1$ cointegrating vectors

Step 4. Compute the test statistic

$$-2\ln(Q) = -T \sum_{i=r+1}^{p} \ln(1 - \lambda_i)$$

where $\lambda_{r+1}, \ldots, \lambda_p$ are the $p - r$ smaller eigenvalues.

Step 5. Obtain the critical value from a chi-square distribution with p degrees of freedom.

Granger-Lee Test

The concept of cointegration between two variables can be extended to the case where additional cointegration may exist with a third variable, which is based on a combination of the first two. Granger and Lee (1990) suggest, for example, that inventories may be cointegrated with consumption or with production, while changes in inventories may be defined by a cointegrating relationship between consumption and production. Recalling the above definition of cointegration, it is generally true for any vector $X(t)$ of N I(1) series, that there will be at most r vectors α such that $\alpha' X(t)$ is I(0), with $r \leq N - 1$. However, it is also true that any pair of I(1) series may be cointegrated and this does allow the possibility of a deeper form of cointegration. Assume that $x(t)$ and $y(t)$ are both I(1), have no trend, and are cointegrated, such that $z(t) = x(t) - \alpha y(t)$ is I(0). Then the following aggregation

$$q(t) = \sum_{j=1}^{t} z(t-j) \tag{3.9}$$

will be I(1), and $x(t)$ and $y(t)$ will be said to be multicointegrated. Note that $q(t)$ represents a cumulative sum of $z(t)$ over all j. If $q(t)$ and $x(t)$ are cointegrated, $q(t)$ and $y(t)$ will also be cointegrated.

Test Procedure

Step 1. Test that each series, $x(t)$, $y(t)$, and $q(t)$ are I(1), for example, using the DF or ADF test.

Step 2. Test that $z(t)$ is I(0), for example, use the DF or ADF test.

Step 3. Estimate the cointegrating regression (3.2) between $q(t)$ and $x(t)$, and $q(t)$ and $y(t)$:

$$q(t) = \alpha_1 + \beta_1 x(t) + u_1(t) \tag{3.10}$$

$$q(t) = \alpha_2 + \beta_2 y(t) + u_2(t) . \tag{3.11}$$

Step 4. Test if the u_i's are I(0), for example, using the DF, ADF, or CRDW test. A result showing I(0) suggests that $z(t)$ is also I(0) and confirms the presence of multicointegration.

Step 5. As a further step in the analysis, error correction models can also be estimated and tested:

$$\Delta x(t) = \alpha + \beta_1 z(t-1) + \beta_2 u_2(t-1) + \beta_3 \Delta x(t-1) + \beta_4 \Delta y(t-1) + v_1(t) \tag{3.12}$$

$$\Delta y(t) = \alpha' + \beta_1' z(t-1) + \beta_2' u_2(t-1) + \beta_3' \Delta x(t-1) + \beta_4' \Delta y(t-1) + v_2(t) \tag{3.13}$$

Note that more than one lag could also be used for x and y on the right-hand side of the equations and that u_2 could have been replaced by u_1. Note that u_1 and u_2 are from Equations 3.10 and 3.11 above. Multicointegration is confirmed by the presence of significant t values on β_2 or β_2'.

Note that the critical values of the ADF test differ from those cited in Fuller (1976) because they refer to the multivariate case. For this type of higher order system, Engle and Yoo (1987) have corrected the ADF values, as reproduced in Appendix Table A.3. The Durbin-Watson test also provides a test of cointegration for the residuals in the equations. For additional information on multicointegration tests and their applications in ECM models, the reader is referred to Granger and Lee (1989) and Labys and Lord (1992).

No numerical example of the Granger-Lee test is provided here because testing for multicointegration requires in practice that $z(t)$ and $q(t)$ are meaningful. This condition was not true for the macropartisanship data employed.

4. TESTING FOR CAUSALITY

In any multivariate setting, researchers are interested in testing for the exogeneity of a variable. Such testing is closely related to the concept of causality due to Granger (1969) and it is often the latter that is used to test for the former. Causality between two or more variables is one of the most important issues that social scientists address in their research. The term *causality* as used here follows Granger's (1969) temporal definition: a variable $x(t)$ *Granger-causes* another variable $y(t)$, if given information of both $x(t)$ and $y(t)$, the variable $y(t)$ can be better predicted in the mean square error sense by using only *past values* of $x(t)$ than by not doing so. In other words, having knowledge of past values of $x(t)$ does improve the ability of the model to predict $y(t)$. We can write this relationship as $x(t) \rightarrow y(t)$. A lesser condition of *instantaneous* causality can also be specified where not only past, but also present values of $x(t)$ improve the ability of the model to predict $y(t)$. Causality from $y(t)$ to $x(t)$ is defined in a like manner.

Feedback occurs in the case where $x(t)$ causes $y(t)$ and $y(t)$ causes $x(t)$. In this case, Pierce and Haugh (1977) demonstrate instantaneous causality under the conditions that $x(t)$ causes $y(t)$ instantaneously, if and only if $y(t)$ causes $x(t)$ instantaneously. There are three possible explanations for apparent instantaneous causality,

  (i) There is true instantaneous causality in the system so that elements in the system react without any measurable time delay to changes in some other elements.
 (ii) There is no true instantaneous causality, but the finite time delay between cause and effect is small, compared to the time interval over which the data is collected.
(iii) There is a jointly causal variable $w(t - 1)$, that causes both $x(t)$ and $y(t)$ but is not included in the information set, possibly because it is not observed.

Consequently, the researcher may wish to determine if a causal relationship exists between $x(t)$ and $y(t)$, if there is reverse causality [i.e., $y(t)$ causing $x(t)$], if there is instantaneous causality, and if feedback occurs between the variables. In any case, the reader is cautioned in the interpretation of causality test results. When we speak of "Granger causality," we are really testing if a particular variable precedes another and not causality in the sense of cause and effect.

In the case where causality testing is interpreted as exogeneity testing, Engle, Hendry, and Richard (1983) have concluded that the two concepts are separate. They prefer to make a distinction between weakly and strongly exogenous variables. The former implies that the exogeneity of the variable does not depend on a variable's importance in predicting other variables, while the latter suggests that a variable is both weakly exogenous and not Granger-caused by any of the other variables.

Various tests for causality have been developed. Most tests not only include the Granger test for causality but also a test for causality in the presence of "leads." Such tests have been developed by Sims, Geweke-Meese-Dent, Pierce-Haugh, and Geweke. It is important to note that for all of these tests it is required that the series being tested are mean-zero stationary series, for example, see Kang (1981, 1985, 1989). For the examples that follow, we will test whether the presidential approval rating (PA) is Granger-caused by the Michigan index of consumer sentiment (MIS). Furthermore, these variables were transformed to first differences of their natural logarithms to minimize heteroscedasticity and to ensure stationarity, unless otherwise stated.

Granger Causality Test

Granger causality reflects the extent to which the lag process in one variable explains the current values of another variable. More formally, we can test the null hypothesis that $x(t)$ does not Granger-cause $y(t)$. In this case, we would employ the following equations:

$$y(t) = \sum_{i=1}^{\infty} \alpha_i y(t-i) + c_1 + v_1(t) \tag{4.1}$$

$$y(t) = \sum_{i=1}^{\infty} \alpha_i y(t-i) + \sum_{j=1}^{\infty} \beta_j x(t-j) + c_2 + v_2(t) \tag{4.2}$$

and test whether $\beta_j = 0$ for all lags j. An F test would be employed where (4.1) is the restricted equation and (4.2) is the unrestricted equation. If the null hypothesis is accepted it indicates that lagged values of $x(t)$ do not significantly explain the variation in $y(t)$, that is, $x(t)$ does *not* Granger-cause $y(t)$.

A similar test would also be conducted to examine whether $y(t)$ does not Granger-cause $x(t)$. The relevant equations in this case are:

$$x(t) = \sum_{i=1}^{\infty} \alpha_i x(t-i) + c_1 + u_1(t) \tag{4.3}$$

$$x(t) = \sum_{i=1}^{\infty} \alpha_i x(t-i) + \sum_{j=1}^{\infty} \beta_j y(t-j) + c_2 + u_2(t) \tag{4.4}$$

Again, one would test whether $\beta_j = 0$ for all j, with (4.3) as the restricted equation and (4.4) as the unrestricted equation in the F test.

The Granger test can also be used to test for *instantaneous* causality between variables, although the reader should be aware that this concept has lesser usefulness. In this case, we wish to examine whether the zero-lag of a given variable is significant in explaining the variation of a second variable. For example, to test the null hypothesis that $x(t)$ does not Granger-cause $y(t)$ instantaneously, we would use the following:

$$y(t) = \sum_{i=1}^{\infty} \alpha_i y(t-i) + \sum_{j=1}^{\infty} \beta_j x(t-j) + c_1 + v_1(t) \tag{4.5}$$

$$y(t) = \sum_{i=1}^{\infty} \alpha_i y(t-i) + \sum_{j=0}^{\infty} \beta_j x(t-j) + c_2 + v_2(t) \tag{4.6}$$

Note that the only difference between these two equations is the definition of j. For the F test, Equation 4.5 would be the restricted equation and (4.6) the unrestricted equation. Similarly, to test if $y(t)$ does not Granger-cause $x(t)$ instantaneously, one would use the following equations:

$$x(t) = \sum_{i=1}^{\infty} \alpha_i x(t-i) + \sum_{j=1}^{\infty} \beta_j y(t-j) + c_1 + u_1(t) \tag{4.7}$$

$$x(t) = \sum_{i=1}^{\infty} \alpha_i x(t-i) + \sum_{j=0}^{\infty} \beta_j y(t-j) + c_2 + u_2(t) \qquad (4.8)$$

where (4.7) is the restricted equation and (4.8) the unrestricted equation for the F test. If the null hypothesis of no causality is rejected in both tests, this would indicate that a "feedback effect" exists between $x(t)$ and $y(t)$. This result is obvious because if $x(t)$ instantaneously causes $y(t)$, then $y(t)$ must also instantaneously cause $x(t)$. Recall that rejecting the null establishes the presence of causality.

It should be stated at this point that feedback among one of the equations still implies a weak form of causality. This results from our inability to separate whether the causality in one direction influences causality in the opposite direction. In addition, if one finds that causality does exist, then the sign as well as the magnitude of the effect of an independent on a dependent variable can be estimated by summing the coefficients in the unrestricted equation on all lags of the independent variable, that is, $\sum \beta_j$. The sign and significance of any particular lag of an independent variable are determined from the t statistic on the coefficient for lag j in the unrestricted equations.

An issue that arises in causality testing is the choice of i and j in the test equations. In many empirical applications, i and j are set equal to each other, that is, the same number of lags of $x(t)$ and $y(t)$ are used in the models. To determine i and j, one would employ a model order test (discussed in Chapter 7) or repeat the causality tests for a range of i and j values. The latter helps to determine if the results remain robust over the lag levels chosen. In practice, the choice of i and j is often rather arbitrary (Pindyck & Rubinfeld, 1976).

Test Procedure

Step 1. Specify the hypotheses to be tested.

Causality Test

H_0: $x(t)$ does not Granger-cause $y(t)$

H_A: $x(t)$ does Granger-cause $y(t)$

H_0: $y(t)$ does not Granger-cause $x(t)$

H_A: $y(t)$ does Granger-cause $x(t)$

Instantaneous Causality Test

H_0: $x(t)$ does not Granger-cause $y(t)$ instantaneously

H_A: $x(t)$ does Granger-cause $y(t)$ instantaneously

H_0: $y(t)$ does not Granger-cause $x(t)$ instantaneously
H_A: $y(t)$ does Granger-cause $x(t)$ instantaneously

Step 2. Assure that the data series are stationary.

Step 3. Choose the number of lags to be used in the equations.

Step 4. Estimate the relevant restricted and unrestricted equations.

Causality Test
For $x(t) \rightarrow y(t)$: Equations 4.1 and 4.2
For $y(t) \rightarrow x(t)$: Equations 4.3 and 4.4

Instantaneous Causality Test
For $x(t) \rightarrow y(t)$: Equations 4.5 and 4.6
For $y(t) \rightarrow x(t)$: Equations 4.7 and 4.8

Step 5. Calculate the test statistic. Note that the formula remains the same for the general causality and the instantaneous causality tests.

$$F = \frac{(ESS_R - ESS_{UR})/q}{ESS_{UR}/(n-k)}$$

Here ESS_R and ESS_{UR} are the error sum of squares for the restricted and unrestricted equations, respectively; q is the number of restrictions applied; n is the total number of observations; and k is the total number of parameters in the unrestricted model (including the constant). The statistic is distributed as an F with q degrees of freedom in the numerator and $n - k$ degrees of freedom in the denominator (i.e., $F_{q, n-k}$).

Step 6. Accept the alternative hypothesis (i.e., Granger-causality) when the calculated F statistic is greater than the critical F value

$$F > F_{q, n-k}.$$

As a final note, recall that the above steps are performed for testing both $x(t) \rightarrow y(t)$ and $y(t) \rightarrow x(t)$, in order to determine any feedback causality relationships.

Example 1. Causality

Step 1. The hypotheses to be tested are:

H_0: MIS(t) does not Granger-cause PA(t)
H_A: MIS(t) does Granger-cause PA(t)
H_0: PA(t) does not Granger-cause MIS(t)
H_A: PA(t) does Granger-cause MIS(t)

Step 2. The data are log transformed and first differenced. They are stationary based on an ADF test.

Step 3. Two lags were chosen for the models based on the fact that longer lags were not significant in the equations. Intuitively, lags longer than 6 months for these variables seem somewhat unlikely.

Step 4. The following restricted and unrestricted equations were estimated:

MIS(t) → PA(t):

Restricted: PA(t) = −0.0018989 + 0.1844146 PA(t − 1)
$\qquad\qquad$ − 0.2805932 PA(t − 2)

Unrestricted: PA(t) = −0.0025044 + 0.0974534 PA(t − 1)
$\qquad\qquad$ − 0.2629668 PA(t − 2) + 0.5730125 MIS(t − 1)
$\qquad\qquad$ + 0.2962459 MIS(t − 2)

PA(t) → MIS(t):

Restricted: MIS(t) = 0.0007425 − 0.073783 MIS(t − 1)
$\qquad\qquad$ + 0.0941276 MIS(t − 2)

Unrestricted: MIS(t) = 0.0005178 − 0.0560708 MIS(t − 1)
$\qquad\qquad$ + 0.1424817 MIS(t − 2) − 0.0589688 PA(t − 1)
$\qquad\qquad$ − 0.0287804 PA(t − 2)

Both sets of equations were estimated for t = 1953.4 − 1988.4.

Step 5. The test statistic is calculated for each pair of hypotheses:

MIS(*t*) → PA(*t*):

$$F = \frac{(1.996747 - 1.824112)/2}{1.824112/(141 - 5)} = 6.436$$

PA(*t*) → MIS(*t*):

$$F = \frac{(0.476405 - 0.467077)/2}{0.467077/(141 - 5)} = 1.358$$

Step 6. The critical F statistics, $F_{2,136}$, are 4.79 at the 1% significance level and 3.07 at the 5% level. Therefore, in the case of MIS(*t*) → PA(*t*) we can accept the alternative hypothesis that MIS does Granger-cause PA. For PA(*t*) → MIS(*t*), we accept the null hypothesis that PA does not Granger-cause MIS.

Example 2. Instantaneous Causality

Step 1. The hypotheses to be tested are:

H_0: MIS(*t*) does not Granger-cause PA(*t*) instantaneously
H_A: MIS(*t*) does Granger-cause PA(*t*) instantaneously
H_0: PA(*t*) does not Granger-cause MIS(*t*) instantaneously
H_A: PA(*t*) does Granger-cause MIS(*t*) instantaneously

Step 2. The data are log transformed and first differenced. They are stationary based on an ADF test.

Step 3. Two lags were chosen for the models based on the fact that longer lags were not significant in the equations.

Step 4. The following restricted and unrestricted equations were estimated:

MIS(*t*) → PA(*t*):

Restricted: PA(*t*) = −0.0025044 + 0.0974534PA(*t* − 1)
　　　　　　− 0.2629668PA(*t* − 2) + 0.5730125MIS(*t* − 1)
　　　　　　+ 0.2962459MIS(*t* − 2)

Unrestricted: $PA(t) = -0.0026902 + 0.1186039PA(t-1)$
$$- 0.25264411PA(t-2) + 0.358674MIS(t)$$
$$+ 0.5931236MIS(t-1) + 0.2451414MIS(t-2)$$

$PA(t) \rightarrow MIS(t)$:

Restricted: $MIS(t) = 0.0005178 - 0.0560708MIS(t-1)$
$$+ 0.1424817MIS(t-2) - 0.0589688PA(t-1)$$
$$- 0.0287804PA(t-2)$$

Unrestricted: $MIS(t) = 0.0007479 - 0.1086969MIS(t-1)$
$$+ 0.1152742MIS(t-2) + 0.0918411PA(t)$$
$$- 0.067919PA(t-1) - 0.0046292PA(t-2)$$

Both sets of equations were estimated for $t = 1953.4 - 1988.4$.

Step 5. The test statistic is calculated for each pair of hypotheses:

$MIS(t) \rightarrow PA(t)$:

$$F = \frac{(1.824112 - 1.7640244)/1}{1.7640244/(141-6)} = 4.599$$

$PA(t) \rightarrow MIS(t)$:

$$F = \frac{(0.467077 - 0.451691)/1}{0.451691/(141-6)} = 4.599$$

Note that for instantaneous causality the F statistics are the same, because the models only differ by the contemporaneous value of the independent variable.

Step 6. The critical F values, $F_{1, 135}$, are 6.85 at the 1% significance level and 3.92 at the 5% level. Therefore, at the 5% level of significance we can accept the alternative hypothesis that MIS and PA cause each other instantaneously. This implies that changes in one variable may lead to changes in the other within the same quarter. This result is not supported at the 1% significance level.

Sims Test

Sims (1972) noted that a necessary condition for $y(t)$ not to Granger-cause $x(t)$ is for future $x(t)$ terms to have zero coefficients in a regression of $y(t)$ on future, current, and lagged values of $x(t)$. As an extension of the Granger causality test, the Sims test includes future values of the independent variable in the unrestricted equation. This test is an attempt to measure *unidirectional* causality. This would imply that although $y(t) \rightarrow x(t)$, the relationship would be passive in the sense that $x(t)$ would not further influence $y(t)$. Sims begins by transforming the natural logarithms of the series $x(t)$ and $y(t)$ according to the filter.

$$x(t)^* = x(t) - 1.5x(t-1) + 0.5625x(t-2) \tag{4.9}$$

This process is purported to flatten the spectral density of many time series and, therefore, to increase the likelihood that the regression residuals are white noise.

To test the null hypothesis that $x(t)$ does not cause $y(t)$, the following equations would be estimated:

$$x(t)^* = \sum_{j=0}^{\infty} \beta_j y(t-j)^* + c_1 + v_1(t) \tag{4.10}$$

$$x(t)^* = \sum_{j=-\infty}^{\infty} \beta_j y(t-j)^* + c_2 + v_2(t) \tag{4.11}$$

where (4.10) would be the restricted equation and (4.11) the unrestricted equation for the F test on the future values of $y(t)^*$.

To test the null hypothesis that $y(t)$ does not cause $x(t)$, the relevant equations would be:

$$y(t)^* = \sum_{j=0}^{\infty} \beta_j x(t-j)^* + c_1 + u_1(t) \tag{4.12}$$

$$y(t)^* = \sum_{j=-\infty}^{\infty} \beta_j x(t-j)^* + c_2 + u_2(t) \tag{4.13}$$

where (4.12) would be the restricted equation and (4.13) the unrestricted equation. In either case, one tests whether $\beta_j = 0$ for all $j < 0$, that is, all future values of the independent variable. Lastly, because both Granger and Sims test the same null hypothesis, the same F test can be employed as in the Granger tests. The reader is referred to Chamberlain (1982) for a comparison of the two methods.

Test Procedure

Step 1. Specify the hypotheses to be tested.

H_0: $x(t)$ does not Granger-cause $y(t)$
H_A: $x(t)$ does Granger-cause $y(t)$
H_0: $y(t)$ does not Granger-cause $x(t)$
H_A: $y(t)$ does Granger-cause $x(t)$

Step 2. Apply Sims's filter procedure to the variables by converting them to natural logarithms and using filter (4.9).

Step 3. Assure that the data are stationary.

Step 4. Choose the number of lags and leads to be used in the models.

Step 5. Estimate the restricted and unrestricted models.

For $x(t) \rightarrow y(t)$: Equations 4.10 and 4.11
For $y(t) \rightarrow x(t)$: Equations 4.12 and 4.13

Step 6. Calculate the test statistic where the values are defined as above (under the Granger test procedure).

$$F = \frac{(\text{ESS}_R - \text{ESS}_{UR})/q}{\text{ESS}_{UR}/(n-k)}$$

Step 7. Accept the alternative hypothesis (i.e., causality) when the calculated F statistic is greater than the critical F value:

$$F > F_{q,\,n-k}.$$

It is important to notice that the placement of $x(t)$ and $y(t)$ in the equations is opposite that for the Granger test.

Example

*Step 1.*The hypotheses to be tested are:

H_0: MIS(t) does not Granger-cause PA(t)
H_A: MIS(t) does Granger-cause PA(t)
H_0: PA(t) does not Granger-cause MIS(t)
H_A: PA(t) does Granger-cause MIS(t)

Step 2. Sims's filter was applied to the data as discussed above.

Step 3. ADF tests were applied to the transformed series showing that differencing was not necessary for stationarity.

Step 4. Based on an examination of the significance of coefficients, two leads and lags were chosen for the models.

Step 5. The restricted and unrestricted models are estimated with the following results:

MIS(t) → PA(t):

Restricted: MIS(t) = 0.3159114 + 0.0027899PA(t)
$\qquad\qquad\quad - 0.0883175\text{PA}(t - 1) - 0.0636508\text{PA}(t - 2)$

Unrestricted: MIS(t) = 0.2589145 + 0.045626PA(t)
$\qquad\qquad\qquad - 0.0456474\text{PA}(t - 1) - 0.0404832\text{PA}(t - 2)$
$\qquad\qquad\qquad + 0.1009578\text{PA}(t + 1) + 0.0193143\text{PA}(t + 2)$

PA(t) → MIS(t):

Restricted: PA(t) = −0.2055766 + 0.5349966MIS(t)
$\qquad\qquad\quad + 0.797695\text{MIS}(t - 1) + 0.3002026\text{MIS}(t - 2)$

Unrestricted: PA(t) = 0.0810658 + 0.3501046MIS(t)
$\qquad\qquad\qquad + 0.8196546\text{MIS}(t - 1) + 0.3926824\text{MIS}(t - 2)$
$\qquad\qquad\qquad - 0.4534611\text{MIS}(t + 1) - 0.5045695\text{MIS}(t + 2)$

Both sets of equations were estimated for $t = 1954.1 - 1988.2$.

Step 6. The F test statistics are calculated as follows:

MIS$(t) \rightarrow$ PA(t):

$$F = \frac{(0.619427 - 0.602454)/2}{0.602454/(138 - 6)} = 1.859$$

PA$(t) \rightarrow$ MIS(t):

$$F = \frac{(2.117792 - 2.003066)/2}{2.003066/(138 - 6)} = 3.780$$

Step 7. The critical F values, $F_{2,138}$ are 4.79 at the 1% significance level and 3.07 at the 5% level. At the 5% level we can accept the alternative hypothesis that PA does cause MIS. At either significance level, however, we accept the null hypothesis that MIS does not cause PA.

Geweke-Meese-Dent Test

In evaluating the above two tests, Geweke, Meese, and Dent (1983) examined a number of forms of causality and found that the Sims test may suffer difficulties because of its failure to correct for serially correlated residuals. As an alternative, they proposed a similar two-sided distributed lag model, but then augmented it with lagged dependent variables to correct for serial correlation. Their modification would not require that the variables be filtered (as in Sims) but only that lags of the dependent variable be added to the equations. Like the previous tests it is also required that the data be stationary. Therefore, to test the null hypothesis that $x(t)$ does not cause $y(t)$, the following equations would be relevant:

$$x(t) = \sum_{i=1}^{\infty} \alpha_i x(t-i) + \sum_{j=0}^{\infty} \beta_j y(t-j) + c_1 + u_1(t) \qquad (4.14)$$

$$x(t) = \sum_{i=1}^{\infty} \alpha_i x(t-i) + \sum_{j=-\infty}^{\infty} \beta_j y(t-j) + c_2 + u_2(t) \qquad (4.15)$$

where (4.14) would be the restricted equation and (4.15) the unrestricted equation for the F test.

Likewise, for the null hypothesis that $y(t)$ does not cause $x(t)$, the relevant equations would be:

$$y(t) = \sum_{i=1}^{\infty} \alpha_i y(t-i) + \sum_{j=0}^{\infty} \beta_j x(t-j) + c_1 + v_1(t) \qquad (4.16)$$

$$y(t) = \sum_{i=1}^{\infty} \alpha_i y(t-i) + \sum_{j=-\infty}^{\infty} \beta_j x(t-j) + c_2 + v_2(t) \qquad (4.17)$$

where Equation 4.16 is the restricted equation for the F test and (4.17) the unrestricted equation. As with the Sims test, one is effectively testing if $\beta_j = 0$ for all $j < 0$, that is, for all future values of the independent variable.

Test Procedure

Step 1. Specify the hypotheses to be tested.

H_0: $x(t)$ does not Granger-cause $y(t)$
H_A: $x(t)$ does Granger-cause $y(t)$
H_0: $y(t)$ does not Granger-cause $x(t)$
H_A: $y(t)$ does Granger-cause $x(t)$

Step 2. Assure that the data are stationary.

Step 3. Choose the number of lags and leads to be used in the equations.

Step 4. Estimate the restricted and unrestricted models.

For $x(t) \rightarrow y(t)$: Equations 4.14 and 4.15
For $y(t) \rightarrow x(t)$: Equations 4.16 and 4.17

Step 5. Calculate the test statistic:

$$F = \frac{(\text{ESS}_R - \text{ESS}_{UR})/q}{\text{ESS}_{UR}/(n-k)}$$

where the values are defined as above.

Step 6. Accept the alternative hypothesis (i.e., causality) when the calculated F statistic is greater than the critical F value:

$$F > F_{q, n-k}.$$

Example

Step 1. The hypotheses to be tested are:

H_0: MIS(t) does not Granger-cause PA(t)
H_A: MIS(t) does Granger-cause PA(t)
H_0: PA(t) does not Granger-cause MIS(t)
H_A: PA(t) does Granger-cause MIS(t)

Step 2. The series were transformed as the first difference of logarithms to minimize heteroscedasticity and to ensure stationarity.

Step 3. Based on an examination of the significance of coefficients, two leads and lags were chosen for the models.

Step 4. The restricted and unrestricted equations are estimated with the following results:

MIS(t) → PA(t):

Restricted: MIS(t) = 0.0009162 + 0.0926212PA(t)
$\qquad$ − 0.0665602PA(t − 1) − 0.0046685PA(t − 2)
$\qquad$ − 0.1082894MIS(t − 1) + 0.1136566MIS(t − 2)

Unrestricted: MIS(t) = 0.0012902 + 0.0932516PA(t)
$\qquad$ − 0.0214257PA(t − 1) + 0.0091303PA(t − 2)
$\qquad$ − 0.1512134MIS(t − 1) + 0.0716905MIS(t − 2)
$\qquad$ + 0.1205712PA(t + 1) + 0.0504747PA(t + 2)

PA(t) → MIS(t):

Restricted: PA(t) = −0.0035822 + 0.3611402MIS(t)
$\qquad$ + 0.5876741MIS(t − 1) + 0.2355088MIS(t − 2)
$\qquad$ + 0.1179491PA(t − 1) − 0.2524594PA(t − 2)

Unrestricted: $PA(t) = -0.0030365 + 0.3854368MIS(t)$
$+ 0.6338273MIS(t-1) + 0.2483188MIS(t-2)$
$+ 0.1383529PA(t-1) - 0.2501703PA(t-2)$
$- 0.1776146MIS(t+1) - 0.3259369MIS(t+2)$

Step 5. The F test statistics are calculated as follows:

MIS(*t*) → PA(*t*):

$$F = \frac{(0.450378 - 0.414041)/2}{0.414041/(139-8)} = 5.748$$

PA(*t*) → MIS(*t*):

$$F = \frac{(1.756073 - 1.696943)/2}{1.696943/(139-8)} = 2.280$$

Step 6. The critical F values, $F_{2,131}$, are 4.79 at the 1% significance level and 3.07 at the 5% level. The results show that the alternative hypothesis that MIS causes PA is accepted at the 1% level, while the null hypothesis that PA does not cause MIS is accepted at either significance level.

This result is consistent with the Granger-causality test results indicating that the Sims test results may have been affected by serial correlation. It should also be noted that this test procedure was also performed with the Sims filtered data, with results consistent to those reported here.

Pierce-Haugh Test

The causal pattern between two variables can be expressed in terms of the cross-correlation functions. For example, define the cross correlation between a pair of series $x(t)$ and $y(t)$ as follows:

$$\rho_{uv}(k) = E[u(t-k)v(t)]/\{E[u^2(t)]E[v^2(t)]\}^{1/2} \qquad (4.18)$$

where $u(t)$ and $v(t)$ are white noise processes of $x(t)$ and $y(t)$, respectively, and k is the number of cross-correlations tested. In practice, we replace (4.18) with the sample cross-correlation function:

$$r_{uv} = \sum u(t-k)v(t)/[\sum u^2(t) \sum v^2(t)]^{1/2} \qquad (4.19)$$

where all terms are defined as above. Pierce and Haugh (1977) transform this sample cross-correlation into the following statistic

$$U = T \sum_{k=-N}^{M} r_{uv}^2(k) \tag{4.20}$$

where T is the number of observations and k is the lag length chosen for the test. Under the null hypothesis that $x(t)$ does not cause $y(t)$, one estimates (4.20) for $k = 1$ to M. The null hypothesis is rejected if U is greater than the selected critical value from a chi-square distribution with $N + M + 1$ degrees of freedom. The null hypothesis that $y(t)$ does not cause $x(t)$ utilizes the U statistic for the values of $k = -1$ to $-M$.

As one can see from the above regressions to be performed, order determination measures must be used to specify the lag length. In addition, residual diagnostics must be performed in order to determine if the residuals resulting from these regressions are strict white noise. Both of these issues are important in order to insure that the above test statistics and critical values are correct.

Test Procedure

Step 1. Specify the hypotheses to be tested:

H_0: $x(t)$ does not cause $y(t)$
H_A: $x(t)$ does cause $y(t)$

and

H_0: $y(t)$ does not cause $x(t)$
H_A: $y(t)$ does cause $x(t)$

Step 2. Filter the series to be white noise. This can be done by obtaining the residuals for the series regressed on lags of itself.

Step 3. Calculate the cross-correlations between the resulting residuals using Equation 4.19.

Step 4. Calculate the test statistic, U, using Equation 4.20 for the chosen lag length k.

Step 5. Accept the alternative hypothesis of causality when the test statistic U is greater than $\chi^2(N + M + 1)$.

Example

Step 1. Specify the hypotheses to be tested:

H_0: MIS(t) does not cause PA(t)
H_A: MIS(t) does cause PA(t)

and

H_0: PA(t) does not cause MIS(t)
H_A: PA(t) does cause MIS(t)

Step 2. The series were filtered by regressing the natural log of MIS(t) on one lag of itself and the natural log of PA(t) on three lags of itself. The resulting residuals were tested as white noise using the Box-Pierce Q statistic; in both cases the hypothesis of white noise was accepted.

Step 3. The cross-correlations between the resulting residual series were estimated for N and M equal to 8.

Step 4. The test statistic was calculated as follows:

MIS(t) → PA(t):

$$U = T \sum_{k=-1}^{-8} r_{uv}^2 = 141(0.1314) = 18.527$$

PA(t) → MIS(t):

$$U = T \sum_{k=1}^{8} r_{uv}^2 = 141(0.068) = 9.508$$

where u and v refer to the white noise processes of MIS(t) and PA(t), respectively.

Step 5. The critical $\chi^2(9)$ values for either test were 21.67 at the 1% significance level and 16.92 at the 5% level. The results suggest acceptance of the alternative hypothesis that MIS(t) does cause PA(t) at the 5% significance level and acceptance of the null hypothesis that PA(t) does not cause MIS(t).

Geweke Test

Geweke (1982, 1984) further developed tests of causality to examine more explicitly the issues of reversals in linear and instantaneous linear causality and dependence between two variables. In effect, these tests attempt to decompose causality by frequency. For all three cases it is assumed that the series are stationary. Note that for reference purposes the notation that follows is that of Geweke (1982).

(i) Linear Feedback

Geweke's measure of linear feedback for $y(t)$ to $x(t)$, and $x(t)$ to $y(t)$, are, respectively:

$$F_{Y \to X} = \ln(|\Sigma_1|/|\Sigma_2|) \tag{4.21}$$

$$F_{X \to Y} = \ln(|T_1|/|T_2|) \tag{4.22}$$

where Σ_1, Σ_2, T_1, T_2 are the residual variance-covariance matrices from Equations 4.3, 4.4, 4.1, and 4.2, respectively. $|*|$ is the determinant operator and ln is the natural logarithm operator. Because $x(t)$ and $y(t)$ are one-dimensional univariate processes, the variance-covariance matrices are scalars. Thus, if the variances in the restricted and unrestricted equations are the same, then the ln(1) will equal 0 and the statement $y(t)$ does not cause $x(t)$ is equivalent to $F_{Y \to X} = 0$ and vice versa.

(ii) Instantaneous Linear Feedback

A measure of instantaneous linear feedback can be derived similarly as:

$$F_{X.Y} = \ln(|\Sigma_2|/|\Sigma_3|) \tag{4.23}$$

or equivalently

$$F_{Y.X} = \ln(|T_2|/|T_3|) \tag{4.24}$$

such that $F_{X.Y} = F_{Y.X}$. Σ_2 and T_2 are defined as above. Σ_3 and T_3 are the residual variance-covariance matrices from Equations 4.8 and 4.6, respectively.

(iii) Linear Dependence

A third concept, closely related to the idea of linear feedback, is linear dependence. Geweke's measure of dependence between $x(t)$ and $y(t)$ can be most simply derived as the sum of the three types of linear feedback presented earlier:

$$F_{X,Y} = F_{Y \to X} + F_{X \to Y} + F_{X.Y}. \tag{4.25}$$

That is, the level of linear dependence between $x(t)$ and $y(t)$ is the sum of the level of linear feedback from $x(t)$ to $y(t)$ and $y(t)$ to $x(t)$, and the level of instantaneous linear feedback between the two series.

Test Procedure

We will consider the test procedures for each of the above in turn. In all cases it is implicit that the series being tested are stationary. All test statistics are likelihood ratio tests that are distributed chi-squared.

(i) Linear Feedback

Step 1. Specify the hypotheses to be tested.

Feedback from $x(t)$ to $y(t)$:
H_0: $F_{X \to Y} = 0$ [no linear feedback from $x(t)$ to $y(t)$]
H_A: $F_{X \to Y} \neq 0$ [linear feedback from $x(t)$ to $y(t)$]

Feedback from $y(t)$ to $x(t)$:
H_0: $F_{Y \to X} = 0$ [no linear feedback from $y(t)$ to $x(t)$]
H_A: $F_{Y \to X} \neq 0$ [linear feedback from $y(t)$ to $x(t)$]

Note that acceptance of the null hypothesis is the same as finding unidirectional causality in the sense of Granger and Sims.

Step 2. Estimate the relevant equations.

For feedback from $x(t)$ to $y(t)$: Equations 4.1 and 4.2
For feedback from $y(t)$ to $x(t)$: Equations 4.3 and 4.4

Step 3. Calculate the relevant test statistic.

For feedback from $x(t)$ to $y(t)$:

$$nF_{X \to Y} \sim \chi^2(klp)$$

For feedback from $y(t)$ to $x(t)$:

$$nF_{Y \to X} \sim \chi^2(klp)$$

Here n is the number of observations; k is the number of variables comprising the vector $X(t)$; l is the number of variables comprising the vector $Y(t)$, and p is the number of lags on the independent variable in the equation tested under the null hypothesis. Note that in the common case where $x(t)$ and $y(t)$ are univariate series, $k = l = 1$.

Step 4. Compare the test statistic to the critical χ^2 value (with klp degrees of freedom) for a given acceptable level of probability, for example, 10% or 5%. The alternative hypothesis of linear feedback is accepted when the test statistic $> \chi^2(klp)$.

(ii) Instantaneous Linear Feedback

Step 1. Specify the hypotheses to be tested.

H_0: $F_{X.Y} = 0$ [no instantaneous feedback between $x(t)$ and $y(t)$]
H_A: $F_{X.Y} \neq 0$ [instantaneous feedback between $x(t)$ and $y(t)$] or equivalently
H_0: $F_{Y.X} = 0$ [no instantaneous feedback between $x(t)$ and $y(t)$]
H_A: $F_{Y.X} \neq 0$ [instantaneous feedback between $x(t)$ and $y(t)$]

Recall that testing only one of these pairs of hypotheses is necessary because $F_{X.Y} = F_{Y.X}$.

Step 2. Estimate the relevant equations.

For $F_{X.Y}$: Equations 4.4 and 4.8
For $F_{Y.X}$: Equations 4.2 and 4.6

Step 3. Calculate the test statistic.

$$nF_{X.Y} \text{ or } nF_{Y.X} \sim \chi^2(klp)$$

Step 4. Compare the test statistic to the critical χ^2 value (with klp degrees of freedom) for the acceptable level of probability. Accept the alternative hypothesis of instantaneous linear feedback when the test statistic $> \chi^2(klp)$.

(iii) Linear Dependence

Step 1. Specify the hypotheses to be tested.

H_0: $F_{X,Y}=0$ [no linear dependence between $x(t)$ and $y(t)$]
H_A: $F_{X,Y}\neq 0$ [linear dependence between $x(t)$ and $y(t)$]

Step 2. Calculate the measure of linear dependence as specified in Equation 4.25.

Step 3. Calculate the test statistic.

$$nF_{X,Y} \sim \chi^2[kl(2p + 1)]$$

where the values are defined as above.

Step 4. Compare the test statistic to the critical χ^2 acceptance value (with $kl[2p + 1]$ degrees of freedom) for the acceptance level of probability. Accept the alternative hypothesis of linear dependence when the test statistic $> \chi^2[kl(2p + 1)]$.

Example

(i) Linear Feedback

Step 1. The hypotheses to be tested are:

Feedback from MIS(t) to PA(t):
H_0: $F_{\text{MIS} \rightarrow \text{PA}} = 0$ [no linear feedback from MIS(t) to PA(t)]
H_A: $F_{\text{MIS} \rightarrow \text{PA}} \neq 0$ [linear feedback from MIS(t) to PA(t)]

Feedback from PA(t) to MIS(t):
H_0: $F_{\text{PA} \rightarrow \text{MIS}} = 0$ [no linear feedback from PA(t) to MIS(t)]
H_A: $F_{\text{PA} \rightarrow \text{MIS}} \neq 0$ [linear feedback from PA(t) to MIS(t)]

Step 2. The relevant equations are estimated using two lags on the variables with the following results:

MIS(t) → PA(t):

Restricted: $PA(t) = -0.0018989 + 0.1844146PA(t - 1)$
$$- 0.2805932PA(t - 2)$$

Unrestricted: $PA(t) = -0.0025044 + 0.0974534PA(t - 1)$
$$- 0.2629668PA(t - 1) + 0.5730125MIS(t - 1)$$
$$+ 0.2962459MIS(t - 1)$$

PA(t) → MIS(t):

Restricted: $MIS(t) = 0.0007425 - 0.073783MIS(t - 1)$
$$+ 0.0941276MIS(t - 2)$$

Unrestricted: $MIS(t) = 0.0005178 - 0.0560708MIS(t - 1)$
$$+ 0.1424817MIS(t - 2) - 0.0589688PA(t - 1)$$
$$- 0.0287804PA(t - 2)$$

Both sets of equations were estimated for $t = 1953.4 - 1988.4$.

Step 3. The test statistics are calculated as follows:

MIS(t) →PA(t):

$$nF_{MIS \rightarrow PA} = 141 \times \ln(0.142624/0.0130293) = 141(0.09042) = 12.750$$

PA(t) → MIS(t):

$$nF_{PA \rightarrow MIS} = 141 \times \ln(0.0034028/0.0033362) = 141(0.019747) = 2.788$$

Step 4. The critical $\chi^2(2)$ values are 9.21 at the 1% significance level and 5.99 at the 5% level. The results show that the alternative hypothesis of linear feedback from MIS to PA is accepted at the 1% level, while we accept the null hypothesis of no linear feedback from PA to MIS.

(ii) Instantaneous Linear Feedback

Step 1. The hypotheses to be tested are:

H_0: $F_{MIS.PA} = 0$ [no instantaneous feedback between MIS(t) and PA(t)]
H_A: $F_{MIS.PA} \neq 0$ [instantaneous feedback between MIS(t) and PA(t)]

Note that we could have also tested the hypotheses regarding $F_{PA.MIS}$. This is not necessary because both tests would produce the same result.

Step 2. The relevant equations using two lags of the variables are estimated with the following results:

Restricted: PA(t) = $-0.0025044 + 0.0974534$PA($t - 1$)
$\qquad\qquad\quad - 0.2629668$PA($t - 2$) $+ 0.5730125$MIS($t - 1$)
$\qquad\qquad\quad + 0.2962459$MIS($t - 2$)

Unrestricted: PA(t) = $-0.0026902 + 0.1186039$PA($t - 1$)
$\qquad\qquad\qquad - 0.2526441$PA($t - 2$) $+ 0.5931236$MIS($t - 1$)
$\qquad\qquad\qquad + 0.2451414$MIS($t - 2$) $+ 0.358674$MIS(t)

Both equations were estimated for $t = 1953.4 - 1988.4$.

Step 3. The test statistic is calculated as follows:

$$nF_{MIS.PA} = 141 \times \ln(0.0130293/0.0126001) = 141(0.0335) = 4.724 \ .$$

Step 4. The critical $\chi^2(2)$ values are 9.21 at the 1% significance level and 5.99 at the 5% level. The results show that the null hypothesis is accepted that there is no instantaneous linear feedback between MIS and PA. As a confirmation, this test was also performed for $FD_{PA.MIS}$ with the identical result.

(iii) Linear Dependence

Step 1. The hypotheses to be tested are:

H_0: $F_{MIS,PA} = 0$ [no linear dependence between MIS(t) and PA(t)]
H_A: $F_{MIS,PA} \neq 0$ [linear dependence between MIS(t) and PA(t)]

Step 2. The measure of linear dependence is calculated based on the estimates in the above examples:

$$F_{MIS,PA} = 0.09042 + 0.019747 + 0.0335 = 0.143667 .$$

Step 3. The test statistic is calculated as:

$$nF_{MIS,PA} = 141(0.143667) = 20.257 .$$

Step 4. The critical $\chi^2(5)$ values are 15.09 at the 1% significance level and 11.07 at the 5% level. Because the test statistic is greater than the critical values, we can accept the alternative hypothesis that MIS and PA are linearly dependent.

It should be noted that Geweke (1984) extends the above analysis to *conditional* linear feedback and dependence. In this case, measures of feedback and dependence between two series are conditional on a third variable. The reader is referred to that work for further exploration.

General Guidelines

Given the many tests disclosed in this section, which test is the most desirable for testing for the presence of causality? At this point there is no irrevocable evidence that can point to one test over the other. The Granger test seems to dominate the empirical studies because of its ease of implementation. Other tests, however, attempt to overcome some of the underlying testing problems. Judge et al. (1985), for example, suggest that testing based on present and past values of a variable does not include all possible relevant information. In addition, they are concerned with employing linear forecasts instead of nonlinear ones (i.e., normality assumption) as well as using the mean square error criterion as a measure of forecast accuracy. The reader should note that the above causality tests are, in reality, tests of improved fit. For tests that go beyond the sample period, Ashley, Granger, and Schmalensee (1980) offer a test where one examines causality by comparing equation forecasts in the post-sample period. For a comparative study of causality tests the reader is referred to Geweke et al. (1983). For studies that empirically implement the above tests of causality, the reader is referred to Caines, Keng, and Sethi (1981), Feige and Pearce (1979), Labys and Maizels (1993), and Nachane, Nadkarni, and Karnik (1988).

5. MULTIVARIATE
LINEAR MODEL SPECIFICATION

Univariate time series models have the advantage of being able to explain or to predict a variable only on the basis of current, past, and future information. There is no doubt, however, that in the context of the social sciences, the explanatory power of univariate models can be improved by incorporating the political or economic information contained in some related or interacting variable. Traditionally, a multivariate time series model provides an adequate unrestricted approximation to the reduced form of an unknown structural specification of a simultaneous equations system. Under the assumption that an underlying structure exists, Zellner (1979) and Zellner and Palm (1974) have shown that any structural model can be written in the form of a multivariate time series model. Among the different forms that bivariate or multivariate time series models can take, additional or explanatory variables can be exogenous; they can be event determined as in the case of intervention models; or they can embody stochastic variation, as in the case of transfer function models (see Granger, 1990). The selection of such variables is intimately bound up with the time series concepts of cointegration and causality.

The modeling approach followed so far assumes that there is no feedback from the univariate or dependent variable to the independent or explanatory variable(s). Because such an assumption is often untenable in the social sciences, multivariate time series models have been developed, such as vector autoregressive models (VAR), that make no distinction between the dependent and the explanatory variables. Table 5.1 summarizes the actual range of multivariate models suitable for applying the above multivariate tests; these include Transfer Function, Vector Autoregressive, Vector Moving Average, Vector Autoregressive Moving Average, Vector Autoregressive Integrated Moving Average, Bayesian Vector Autoregressive, and Error Correction models.

Transfer Function Models (TF)

In Chapter 4, tests of causality were used to determine exogeneity in the model identification process. Given that Granger instantaneous causality exists in one direction only, a finite parametric linear specification for the stationary bivariate vector $X(t)$ is

TABLE 5.1

Examples of Multivariate Linear Time Series Models Specifications

VAR(p)	$\varphi_p(L)\,X(t) = C + V(t)$
VMA(q)	$X(t) = C + \Theta_q(L)V(t)$
VARMA(p, q)	$\varphi_p(L)\,X(t) = C + \Theta_q(L)V(t)$
VARIMA(p, d, q)	$\varphi_p(L)[1 - L]^d\,X(t) = C + \Theta_q(L)V(t)$
BVAR(p)	$x_i(t) = \displaystyle\sum_{j=1}^{n} \sum_{k=1}^{p} \alpha_{i,jk}\, x_j(t-k) + c_i + V_i(t)$

where

$$\alpha_{i,ik} \sim N\{\delta_{ik},\, \pi_5\pi_1/[k\exp(\pi_4)]\}$$

$$\alpha_{i,jk} \sim N\{0,\, \pi_5\pi_2\sigma_i^2/[k\exp(2\pi_4)\sigma_j^2]\} \quad \text{for } i \ne j$$

$$c_i \sim N(0,\, \pi_5\pi_3\pi_2\sigma_i^2)$$

$$\sum_{i=1}^{p} \alpha_{i,jk} \sim N(\delta_{ij},\, \sigma_j^2/\pi_6 2\sigma_i^2)$$

ECM(p, q)	$\varphi_p(L)[1 - L]\,X(t) = -Az(t-1) + \Theta_q(L)V(t)$

NOTE: The vector $X(t)$ is assumed to be a jointly, second-order stationary vector of variables; C is a vector of constants; d is the order of integration that is the same for each component of the vector, $X(t)$; and residual vector $V(t)$ is assumed to be independent and jointly stationary. π_i are the parameters with the prior for the BVAR model: π_1 is relative tightness on own lags; π_2 is relative tightness of lags of other variables, π_3 is relative tightness on constant term, π_4 is differential tightness among other variables, π_5 is overall tightness, and π_6 is looseness on sums of coefficients. The p is the number of autoregressive lags and q is the number of moving average lags. $z(t-1)$ is the error correction term based on the residuals from the cointegrating regression and L is the lag or backshift operator. Other parameter designations can be found in the text. The models are: Vector Autoregressive (VAR), Vector Moving Average (VMA), Vector Autoregressive Moving Average (VARMA), Vector Autoregressive Integrated Moving Average (VARIMA), Bayesian Vector Autoregressive (BVAR), and Error Correction Model (ECM).

$$x(t) = a_1 x(t-1) + \ldots + a_p x(t-p) + b_0 y(t) + b_1 y(t-1) \qquad (5.1)$$
$$+ \ldots + b_q y(t-q) + v(t)$$

where a_i and b_j are coefficients; $x(t)$ and $y(t)$ are the scalar time series from the vector $X(t)$; and $v(t)$ is an independent and identically distributed residual process. Box and Jenkins (1976) refer to (5.1) as a *transfer function* (TF) model. As stated above, such models are useful for improving the forecasts of future values of $x(t)$ by basing forecasts not only on past values of $x(t)$ but also on past and present values of a related series, $y(t)$.

The transfer function model is a more restricted version of the multivariate version of the univariate autoregressive model. The basic distinction between the two specifications often made by engineers is that multivariate autoregressive models are *closed-loop* systems, as opposed to the *open-loop* systems of transfer function models. Because the multivariate autoregressive specification includes all endogenous variables in each equation, feedback can occur in the system. A transfer function model would be appropriate in those situations where a causal relationship exists between or among variables in a particular direction. If, however, this is not the case and causality exists in both directions, then feedback occurs and a multivariate autoregressive model is more appropriate. Making this choice represents an application of the causality tests of the previous chapter.

Vector Autoregressive Models (VAR)

The vector autoregressive (VAR) model is the multivariate counterpart to the univariate autoregressive model discussed in Chapter 2 of UTM. The vector autoregressive model (VAR) is defined as follows:

$$\Phi_p(L) \, X(t) = V(t) \tag{5.2}$$

where $\Phi_p(L) = (I - A_1L^1 - \ldots - A_pL^p)$ and L^i is the backshift operator such that $L^iX(t) = X(t-1)$ for $i \neq 0$. In this case $\Phi_p(L)$ is the A matrix polynomial in the backshift operator L; k is the number of variables in $X(t)$; I is a $k \times k$ identity matrix; A_i is the $k \times k$ matrix of coefficients; $V(t)$ is a k-dimensional vector of strict white noise, resulting in $E[V(t)] = 0$; and $E[V(t)V(s)']$ is a diagonal, positive definite, variance-covariance matrix Σ_v. If the above process is stationary with the determinant of $\Phi_p(L)$ given by $|\Phi_p(L)| \neq 0$ for $|z| \leq 1$, then the matrix polynomial $\Phi_p(L)$ is invertible and there exists a moving average representation. This is strictly analogous to the invertibility condition in the univariate AR case.

As an example of the above notation, consider the following bivariate VAR(1) process represented in (5.3)

$$x(t) = \alpha_{11} x(t-1) + \alpha_{12} y(t-1) + v_1(t)$$
$$y(t) = \alpha_{21} x(t-1) + \alpha_{22} y(t-1) + v_2(t) \tag{5.3}$$

where $v_1(t)$ and $v_2(t)$ are independent, stationary processes. The coefficient matrix A_1 is defined as

$$A_1 = \begin{bmatrix} \alpha_{11} & \alpha_{12} \\ \alpha_{21} & \alpha_{22} \end{bmatrix}. \tag{5.4}$$

Clearly, only in the case where feedback is confirmed in the Granger causality context can one use VAR models. It is pointed out, however, that instantaneous feedback does not occur in VAR models. Quite often, VAR modeling is conducted without reference to the previous chapter on causality. A detailed treatment of the VAR model can be found in Granger and Newbold (1986), Judge et al. (1985), Litterman (1986), and Sims (1972, 1981). Empirical applications of VAR models are quite numerous. Some examples include Cargill and Morus (1988), Corman, Joyce, and Lovitch (1987), Cromwell and Hannan (1988), Fackler and Krieger (1986), Gruben and Long (1988), Hoehn, Gruben, and Fomby (1984), Kaylen (1988), and Labys, Murcia, and Terraza (1994).

One important aspect of estimating VAR models that cannot be overlooked concerns cointegration and the decision to utilize original series or some transformed version. Engle and Granger (1987) state that vector time series that have cointegrated elements will result in misspecified VARs if the data are differenced. An error correction model can, however, be rewritten as a VAR if the data are in levels.

Vector Moving Average Models (VMA)

The next multivariate model, the vector moving average (VMA) model, constitutes a multivariate extension of the MA model now defined as

$$X(t) = \theta_q(L)V(t) \tag{5.5}$$

where $\theta_q(L) = (I - B_1 L^1 - \ldots - B_q L^q)$. Here L^i is the backshift operator such that $L^i e_t = e_{t-1}$ for $i \neq 0$; $\theta_q(L)$ is the A matrix polynomial in the backshift operator L; I is a $k \times k$ identity matrix; A_i is the $k \times k$ matrix of coefficients; $V(t)$ is a k-dimensional vector of white noise, resulting in $E[V(t)] = 0$; and $E[V(t)V(s)']$ is a diagonal, positive definite, variance-covariance matrix Σ_v. Given that the specification of the matrix polynomial is similar to that of the VAR specification, the VMA model can be obtained from the VAR specification

$$X(t) = \Gamma(L)V(t) \tag{5.6}$$

where $\Gamma(L) = [\Phi_p(L)]^{-1}$ and the process, $X(t)$, in (5.6) is *jointly stationary*.

The motivation for determining the moving average representation of a multivariate autoregressive process has two advantages, estimation and interpretation. The first advantage, estimation, involves the result that least squares is efficient in estimating VAR models as opposed to nonlinear least squares in the estimation of VMA models. The second advantage refers to the use of multivariate time series models as the equivalent of reduced forms of structural models, and the desire of researchers to extract information concerning the dynamic "multipliers" of the system. Sims (1981) has coined the phrase *innovation accounting* to refer to the operation of extracting this information from a VAR model.

Using the terminology of Sims (1981), a *shock* is defined to be a one time unit increase in one of the m variables of the vector $X(t) = [1, 0, \ldots, 0]$ at time $t = 0$. That is, except for the shock variable, all other variables in the vector $X(t)$ are assumed to be zero at time $t = 0$. Therefore, this shock or unit increase in the variable can also be expressed by the initial error or innovation, $V(t) = [1, 0, \ldots, 0]$. This can be traced through the system by examining the matrices of the moving average representation from a VAR specification.

This consists of measuring the response of a system to a series of shocks or innovations. The impact of these shocks can be estimated through the *impulse responses* and the *variance decompositions* of a multivariate system.

Impulse Responses

In order to compute these impulse responses, the moving average coefficients must first be calculated from the coefficients of the VAR model according to

$$\Gamma_j = \sum_{i=1}^{j} \Gamma_{j-i} A_i, \tag{5.7}$$

where Γ_j is from the VMA specification

$$X(t) = \sum_{j=1}^{\infty} \Gamma_j V(t-j) \tag{5.8}$$

and where j is defined as above. Also, $\Gamma_0 = I_k$ is a $k \times k$ identity matrix, and $A_i = 0$ for $i > p$. As an example, assume that the accepted VAR model is p

= 1. In this case, the impulse responses or the moving average coefficients can be derived from (5.7) as follows

$$\text{(i)} \quad \Gamma_1 = \Gamma_0 A_1 = A_1$$

$$\text{(ii)} \quad \Gamma_2 = \Gamma_1 A_1 + \Gamma_0 A_2 = A_1^2 \qquad (5.9)$$

$$\text{(iii)} \quad \Gamma_3 = \Gamma_2 A_1 + \Gamma_1 A_2 + \Gamma_0 A_3 = A_1^3$$

The interpretation of an impulse response to the variable $x_1(t)$ is that it responds to a shock or increase in the variance of another variable, $x_2(t)$. If we make the shock equal to one standard deviation, then the coefficient in the matrix (i) gives the magnitude of the response. Through the recursive formula in (5.7) we can obtain the magnitude of the response after n periods. It is important to note that the shock is a one time event. Thus, if the process is stationary, successive powers on A (i.e., after n periods) causes the magnitude of the response to approach zero.

Differences exist in impulse applications between a one-time standard error shock and one-time unit shock. The standard error shock does not consider the contemporaneous correlations between the residuals of Equation 5.2 and thus relates the size of the shock to the fit of the equation. In contrast, the unit shock introduces an orthogonalization that eliminates the contemporaneous residual correlations. By diagonalizing the residual matrix, this has the effect of making some variables act exogenously in order to remove the contemporaneous correlation of the residuals between equations. Orthogonalization is also another way of identifying the model by placing restrictions on the covariance matrix instead of restricting lag lengths. To measure the impacts of these shocks, the Choleski factorization is often used in the estimation of impulse responses. The ordering of the variables to be examined thus depends on the nature of the behavioral questions posed and on the structure of the covariance matrix of residuals. Because of the *nonuniqueness* of the impulse responses with respect to this ordering, some other form of a rationale must be imposed. One rationale is to use the causality testing procedure of Chapter 4, or one can use the variance decompositions.

Variance Decompositions

One often used approach for determining the ordering of the variables is to partition the variance of the forecast error into proportions attributable to the innovations of each variable in the system. The variance decompositions can be defined as the percentage of variance of the h-step forecast of variable k due to innovations in variable j:

$$w_{kj,h} = \sum_{i=0}^{h-1} (e_k'\varphi_i e_j)^2 / \mathrm{MSE}_k(h) . \tag{5.10}$$

Here $i = 0$ to $h - 1$ and $\mathrm{MSE}_k(h) = \sum e_k' \Gamma_i \sum_e \Gamma_i' e_k$; e_k is the kth column of I_k; φ_i is the matrix of orthogonalized impulse responses; and $\mathrm{MSE}_k(h)$ is the mean squared error (forecast error variance) of an h-step forecast of variable k. Thus, both the orthogonalized and unorthogonalized impulse responses are included in the variance decomposition measure.

Sims (1981) has made the following suggestions as to how the variables might be ordered in order to obtain the impulses.

(i) Variables that are not expected to have any predictive value for other variables should be put last. For example, if one were examining local and national linkages, one would not expect local variables to explain national ones. Therefore, the local variables would be placed last.

(ii) The first variable in the ordering explains 100% of its first-step variance. If this does not occur, then some contemporaneous correlation exists in the residuals of the variables in the ordering.

One test of exogeneity would be to place a variable first in the ordering and use Sim's remarks as a guideline. As an alternative, one can fit a linear specification to the vector of residuals from the VAR specification and use these parameters to adjust the impulse responses. As Cromwell and Hannan (1993) suggest, decompositions implicitly induce a weighing scheme on impulse response functions.

Testing Decompositions and Impulse Functions

Because the impulse functions are nothing more than moving average coefficients, standard tests of significance can be applied as in the moving average model. Because the coefficients are not directly estimated, however, empirical tests of significance of impulse responses and variance decompositions have been conducted through confidence interval estimation. There are three techniques commonly used to construct confidence intervals. One can begin by using the Monte Carlo integration method based on normality of the residuals (Kloek & Van Dijk, 1978). A second method deals with bootstrapping a mean and variance from the empirical distribution of the residuals (Efron, 1982). The third method is based on asymptotic normal approximations of the error process (Lutkepohl, 1990; Runkle, 1987).

Confidence interval generation using these methods may be limited. Because the process is stationary, the impulses taper off to zero as the number of impulses, i, becomes large. This is reasonable, because one would expect that the effect of a shock on an exogenous variable should logically move toward zero over time. In other words, if a system is shocked from equilibrium at $t = 0$, then over time the system should return to equilibrium at some future period. If the error vector is assumed as $t = 0$, then it should return to zero at some future point also. Furthermore, Lutkepohl (1990) states that if the vector time series is jointly stationary in a VAR model with a finite number of lags, the probability is near 1 that the impulse response values are close to zero as i increases. Intuitively, a test of the null hypothesis that the impulse is zero for large i should be accepted. Standard practice is to exploit the assumption of a symmetric distribution and to generate confidence intervals using the empirical rule, for example, of two standard deviations for a 95% confidence interval. Quite often, at the empirical level the above result is violated. Recently, Lutkepohl (1989, 1990) developed a Wald test based on normal approximations for implementing a test of significance for the impulse responses.

The actual process of estimating VAR models, including the impulse responses and variance decompositions, can be viewed in the following example, which also shows the versatility of MicroTSP in this regard.

Example

Step 1. For the period 1953.4 to 1988.4, a VAR(2) model is estimated for the ΔMIS and ΔMACRO variables. As was demonstrated in the section on cointegration, both MIS and MACRO are I(1) variables, which are also not cointegrated. The MicroTSP output consists of one table for each variable (see Table 5.2).

Step 2. From the VAR estimates in Step 1, the orthogonalized impulse response functions are calculated for eight time periods (see Table 5.3). Because the vector is bivariate, the ordering does not make a difference in the results.

TABLE 5.2
Example of a VAR(2) Model

VAREST / / Dependent Variable is ΔMIS
Date: 8-20-1993 / Time: 8:07
SMPL range: 1953.4 - 1988.4
Number of observations: 141

VARIABLE	COEFFICIENT	STD. ERROR	T-STAT.	2-TAIL SIG.
ΔMIS(−1)	−0.0111240	0.0851827	−0.1305901	0.8963
ΔMIS(−2)	0.1434281	0.0847162	1.6930430	0.0927
ΔMACRO(−1)	37.600545	21.879607	1.7185202	0.0880
ΔMACRO(−2)	6.3048989	22.300652	0.2827226	0.7778
C	0.0705894	0.3723548	0.1895755	0.8499

R-squared	0.039085	Mean of dependent var	0.063121
Adjusted R-squared	0.010823	S.D. of dependent var	4.444702
S.E. of regression	4.420585	Sum of squared resid	2657.654
Log likelihood	−407.0893	F-statistic	1.382939
Durbin-Watson stat	2.032082	Prob(F-statistic)	0.243107

VAREST / / Dependent Variable is ΔMACRO
Date: 8-20-1993 / Time: 8:07
SMPL range: 1953.4 - 1988.4
Number of observations: 141

VARIABLE	COEFFICIENT	STD. ERROR	T-STAT.	2-TAIL SIG.
ΔMIS(−1)	−0.0002664	0.0003268	−0.8150768	0.4165
ΔMIS(−2)	−0.0006105	0.0003250	−1.8781570	0.0625
ΔMACRO(−1)	−0.1732329	0.0839473	−2.0635897	0.0410
ΔMACRO(−2)	−0.1492255	0.0855628	−1.7440461	0.0834
C	−3.768E−05	0.0014286	−0.0263747	0.9790

R-squared	0.065726	Mean of dependent var	−2.16E−05
Adjusted R-squared	0.038247	S.D. of dependent var	0.017295
S.E. of regression	0.016961	Sum of squared resid	0.039123
Log likelihood	377.3107	F-statistic	2.391880
Durbin-Watson stat	2.001390	Prob(F-statistic)	0.053727

Residual Covariance Matrix

1,1	18.84861	1,2	−0.006545	2,2	0.000277

Residual Correlation Matrix

1,1	1.000000	1,2	−0.090500	2,2	1.000000

Step 3. In addition to the impulse responses, variance decompositions are calculated for eight time periods (see Table 5.4).

Steps 2 and 3 provide the MicroTSP 7.0 output of the impulse response and variance decomposition procedure. Interpretation of the magnitude is

TABLE 5.3

Example of Impulse Responses

Response of ΔMIS to One Standard Deviation Shocks

Period	ΔMIS	ΔMACRO
1	4.341498	0.000000
2	-0.104978	0.623757
3	0.580689	-0.010402
4	-0.111474	-0.009148
5	0.086612	0.000968
6	-0.016673	0.010948
7	0.011892	-0.002205
8	-0.003979	5.03E-05

Response of ΔMACRO to One Standard Deviation Shocks

Period	ΔMIS	ΔMACRO
1	-0.001507	0.016589
2	-0.000895	-0.002874
3	-0.002242	-0.002144
4	0.000431	0.000422
5	-6.49E-05	0.000256
6	-8.16E-06	-0.000102
7	-3.73E-05	-2.40E-05
8	1.47E-05	1.33E-05

difficult due to the orthogonalization of the variance-covariance matrix; however, the timing of the impacts is acyclic in terms of the response of ΔMIS to a shock in ΔMACRO. In Step 3 the decompositions should be interpreted such that in the first period, close to 100% of the variance is due to the variance decomposition of that variable. If for some reason this did not occur, then significant correlation would exist between the residuals of the VAR specification. Unfortunately, as can be seen in both panels of Table 5.4, each variable explains very little variance of the other variable.

Bayesian Vector Autoregressive Models (BVAR)

One of the problems faced in VAR modeling is that of multicollinearity. For example, examine the VAR model presented in the example. Clearly, inspection of the t statistics of the different lag coefficients indicates that certain lags of the variables do not belong in certain equations. Inclusion of these "un-necessary" lags or coefficients could result in a multicollinearity problem. The usual approach to this degrees-of-freedom problem is to

TABLE 5.4
Example of Variance Decompositions

Variance Decomposition of ΔMIS

Period	S.E.	ΔMIS	ΔMACRO
1	4.341498	100.0000	0.000000
2	4.387334	97.97871	2.021294
3	4.425609	98.01296	1.987036
4	4.427022	98.01381	1.986194
5	4.427869	98.01456	1.985439
6	4.427914	98.01398	1.986010
7	4.427930	98.01398	1.986020
8	4.427932	98.01398	1.986018

Variance Decomposition of ΔMACRO

Period	S.E.	ΔMIS	ΔMACRO
1	0.016657	0.819029	99.18097
2	0.016927	1.072931	98.92707
3	0.017209	2.735850	97.26415
4	0.017220	2.795267	97.20473
5	0.017222	2.796033	97.20397
6	0.017222	2.795957	97.20404
7	0.017222	2.796408	97.20359
8	0.017222	2.796477	97.20352

reduce the number of regressors, which in autoregressive models means using fewer lags or excluding variables. This would result in changing the specification to a transfer function or simultaneous equation model. On the other hand, dropping a lag in effect forces its coefficients to zero.

Rather than adopting this all-or-nothing approach, Litterman (1986) has observed that coefficients on longer lags are more likely to be close to zero than they are on shorter lags. Using this information in a Bayesian context, normal prior distributions with means of zero and small standard deviations should be placed on the longer lags. Given the difficulties of accomplishing this task, Litterman (1986) imposed the following priors on the coefficients of a VAR model:

$$x_i(t) = \sum_{j=1}^{n} \sum_{k=1}^{p} \alpha_{i,jk} x_j(t-k) + c_i + V_i(t) \tag{5.11}$$

where

$$\alpha_{i,ik} \sim N\{\delta_{ik}, \pi_5\pi_1/[k\exp(\pi_4)]\}$$

$$\alpha_{i,jk} \sim N\{0, \pi_5\pi_2\sigma_i^2/[k\exp(2\pi_4)\sigma_j^2]\} \quad \text{for } i \neq j$$

$$c_i \sim N(0, \pi_5\pi_3\pi_2\sigma_i^2)$$

$$\sum_{i=1}^{p} \alpha_{i,jk} \sim N(\delta_{ij}, \sigma_j^2/\pi_6 2\sigma_i^2)$$

The parameters π_i are associated with the priors for the BVAR model: π_1 is the relative tightness on own lags; π_2 is the relative tightness on lags of other variables; π_3 is the relative tightness on constant term; π_4 is the differential tightness among other variables; π_5 is the overall tightness; π_6 is the looseness on sums of coefficients; and p is the number of autoregressive lags.

Estimation of this model is accomplished through Theil's mixed estimation procedure. RATS 3.0 has an existing routine for estimation of BVAR models and Doan (1988) gives a detailed explanation of estimation procedures for the BVAR model. For a detailed explanation of the model the reader is referred to Doan (1988), Doan, Litterman, and Sims (1984), and Litterman (1986); for empirical implementation consult Cromwell and Hannan (1988) and Litterman (1984).

Vector Autoregressive Moving Average Models (VARMA)

The vector autoregressive moving average model (VARMA) is a multivariate representation of univariate ARMA models discussed in UTM. A VARMA representation of a joint stationary vector $X(t)$ appears as:

$$\Phi_p(L)X(t) = \theta_q(L)V(t) . \tag{5.12}$$

Here $\Phi_p(L) = (I - A_1L^1 - \ldots - A_pL^p)$ and $\theta_q(L) = (I + B_1L^1 + \ldots + B_qL^q)$; L is the backshift operator such that $L^iX(t) = X(t-1)$ for $i \neq 0$; $\Phi_p(L)$ and $\theta_q(L)$ are the matrix polynomials in the backshift operator L; I is a $k \times k$ identity matrix; and p and q are the orders of the autoregressive and moving average components, respectively.

One major problem of VARMA models and restricted models in this class (e.g., VAR, VMA and BVAR) is that of nonuniqueness. As Judge et al. (1985) suggest, two different vector ARMA models can also represent a vector time series process with identical covariance matrices. This corresponds to the identification problem for simultaneous equation models. Typically, uniqueness is established by determining the order for both the autoregressive and moving average operators. Because estimation of VARMA models involves the use of nonlinear least squares procedures, one can utilize the multivariate version of Wold's Decomposition Theorem (e.g., Hannan, 1970), which permits the identification of a VAR representation for the vector time series.

As an extension of the VARMA specification, vector autoregressive integrated moving average models (VARIMA) are the multivariate equivalent of the univariate ARIMA models discussed in UTM. The reader is referred to Hannan (1970), Judge et al. (1985), Mills (1990), Quenouille (1957), and Riise and Tjostheim (1985) for a detailed discussion.

Error Correction Models (ECM)

As illustrated in Figure 5.1, if one knows that the vector $X(t)$ has cointegrated components, then the above list of models will cause specification problems. As an alternative, the error correction model improves the explanatory power between one time series variable and another by including a correction based on the observed deviations between these variables. In order adequately to explain the structure and facilitate the development of an error correction model (ECM), one can draw upon the concept of cointegration explained earlier. Recall the cointegrating regression given by (3.1)

$$x(t) - \alpha y(t) = e(t) . \tag{5.13}$$

In the general case, cointegration exists where $x(t)$ and $y(t)$ have integration order d,b where d is the order of integration and $b > 0$, such that $e(t)$ is I($d - b = 0$).

Granger (1981, 1986) has demonstrated that a relationship exists between cointegration and error correction models; this is specified in his representation theorem as summarized below.

Granger Representation Theorem. If the vector time series $X(t)$ is cointegrated CI(1,1) with cointegrating rank r, then:

(i)   C(1) is of rank $N - r$.
(ii) There exists a vector ARMA representation.

(iii) There exists an error correction representation.

(iv) If a finite VAR model is possible, it will have the form similar to that of (ii) and (iii).

Condition (iii) states, for example, that in the bivariate case of $x(t)$ and $y(t)$, which are both I(1) and cointegrated, there exists an "error correcting form"

$$(1 - L)x(t) = -\rho_1 e(t - 1) + \text{lagged}[(1 - L)x(t), (1 - L)y(t)] + d(L)v_1(t)$$

$$(1 - L)y(t) = -\rho_2 e(t - 1) + \text{lagged}[(1 - L)x(t), (1 - L)y(t)] + d(L)v_2(t)$$

$$(5.14)$$

where $e(t) = x(t) - \alpha y(t)$. The finite polynomial in the lag operator L, $d(L)$, is the same for each equation, and $v_1(t)$ and $v_2(t)$ are joint white noise with $|\rho_1| + |\rho_2| \neq 0$. If we take $d(L)$ equal to 1, then (5.14) becomes a VAR(p) specification with the added term $e(t - 1)$ in each equation. Note that if one has an error correction model, there must be causality in at least one direction via the error correction terms. In addition, there may be causality through the lagged differences.

Granger (1986) states that it is possible to have nonlinear cointegration by reformulating the model to allow the term $e(t - 1)$ to enter the process nonlinearly. For example, the specification of the error correction model in the bivariate case would be

$$(1 - L)x(t) = f_1[e(t - 1)] + \text{lagged}[(1 - L)x(t), (1 - L)y(t)] + v_1(t)$$

$$(1 - L)y(t) = f_2[e(t - 1)] + \text{lagged}[(1 - L)x(t), (1 - L)y(t)] + v_2(t)$$

$$(5.15)$$

where $e(t) = x(t) - \alpha y(t)$. Granger (1986) states that it is generally true that if $e(t)$ is I(0), then any function of $e(t)$, $f[e(t)]$, will be I(0). Generally, $e(t)$ and $f[e(t)]$ will be integrated of the same order. If a test suggests that a pair of series are cointegrated, then the nonlinear error-correction model of (5.15) is a possibility.

In order to estimate the ECM, a two-step procedure is employed (Engle & Granger, 1987). First, a prior regression is performed, called the cointegrating regression; this allows the hypothesis of cointegration to be tested. If cointegration is found to be present, the residuals from this regression are then entered into the ECM specification in place of the series in levels. This intuitively has the effect of imposing a set of parameter values on the level regression that give ordinary least squares (OLS) errors for this step.

Both steps require using the OLS method equation by equation, and Granger (1987) has shown that this procedure yields consistent parameter estimates.

The importance of this procedure is that if the levels part of the ECM is not made up of a cointegrated vector, then this part of the error term will be nonstationary (see Chapter 3). Unless there is an exactly offsetting nonstationarity coming from the difference terms in the equation, the overall ECM error term will also be nonstationary. In order to estimate a valid ECM model for the vector X we must, therefore, include the full cointegrating vector in the level part of the model.

Examples of studies that present ECM models are Granger (1986), Hall (1986), Labys and Lord (1992), and Lesage (1990a, 1990b).

State-Space Models

Although VAR and VARMA models can be easily interpreted and are convenient for evaluating theories and forecasting, an alternative model representation exists that can be productively employed in the multivariate context. Of primary importance is the notion of a "state change" and its embodiment into a "state-space" representation. This state-space form can be explained in terms of a multivariate time series, $X(t)$, containing m elements. Assume that a $m \times 1$ vector of observations $X(t)$ can be written in the form of an *observation equation*

$$X(t) = A(t)' Z(t) + V(t) \qquad (5.16)$$

where $t = 1, 2, \ldots, T$. Here $A(t)$ is an $m \times k$ matrix of coefficients that specifies how the unobserved state vector $Z(t)$, also an $m \times k$ matrix known as the *state vector,* can be translated into the observation vector $X(t)$ at any time point t. The residual vector $V(t)$ is assumed to be a white noise process; it is independent with a zero mean vector and constant covariance matrix R, that is, $R = E[V(t)V(t)']$.

Determination of the behavior of the state vector results from its initial value $Z(0)$, which is assumed to be a random variable; the corresponding *state equations* are given by

$$Z(t) = \Phi Z(t - 1) + W(t) \qquad (5.17)$$

for $t = 1, \ldots, T$, where Φ is a $k \times k$ *transition matrix* and $W(t)$ is another white noise vector that is assumed to be independent of $V(t)$. The covariance matrix of $W(t)$ is denoted by Q, that is, $Q = E[W(t)W(t)']$. In order to complete the specification, assume that the initial vector $Z(0)$ has a constant mean vector, μ, and covariance matrix denoted by Σ.

Model application requires identifying and estimating the state vector $Z(t)$ and the unknown parameters, μ, Σ, Φ, Q, and R. Under the assumption that these parameters are known, the problem of estimating $Z(t)$ recursively can be solved by using a method proposed by Kalman (1960), known as the *Kalman filter*.

One distinct advantage of the specification as opposed to the VAR models is that restrictions for stationarity need not be imposed here. This allows the state-space representation to have greater flexibility in modeling. Further discussion of the properties of this model can be found in Granger and Newbold (1986) and in Harvey (1990). An empirical application to time series appears in Labys, Nakkar, and Terraza (1993).

6. MULTIVARIATE NONLINEAR MODELS

As previously discussed in Chapter 7 of UTM, model specification involves finding a functional representation that reduces a variable to white noise. In the multivariate context, this can simply be written as

$$F[X(t \pm 1), X(t \pm 1), \ldots, X(t \pm 1)] = V(t) \qquad (6.1)$$

where $X(t)$ is an m-dimensional vector of variables and $V(t)$ is an m-dimension vector of white noise residuals. Up to now our attention has focused on the linear specification of the function F. However, the possibility also exists to consider a nonlinear specification. Although the specification, identification, and estimation of this general class of models has been slow to develop, there do exist three classes of specification that have recently grown in popularity in an attempt to model nonlinear dependence.

The first obvious way to incorporate nonlinearity into a model is to vary the parameters of a linear model, such as VAR, in the manner of a random coefficient model (e.g., Cooley & Prescott, 1973). This model fits nicely into the multivariate linear framework discussed in the previous chapter. Random coefficient or varying parameter models can be specified and estimated for VAR, VARMA, BVAR, State-Space, and ECM models. The reader is referred to Doan et al. (1984) for an application of the varying parameter framework to the BVAR model, which includes impulse response function and variance decomposition methods.

The second approach is to generalize the univariate nonlinear models presented in UTM to a multivariate setting. Unfortunately, at this point little work has been conducted regarding the identification and estimation of these models. One exception is Subba Rao (1981) and Granger and Andersen (1978), who have defined a multivariate extension of bilinear time series models and discuss their related statistical properties.

The third approach is to utilize a specification that has become increasingly popular in the artificial intelligence literature (e.g., Werbos, 1974). Artificial neural networks provide a vehicle whereby one can examine a general nonlinear specification of (6.1) without reference to an exact specification.

Feedforward Neural Networks

Artificial neural networks are models that attempt to mimic the way the brain processes information. Because the brain is a highly nonlinear system, it is reasonable to extend the specification of these models to the multivariate time series context. One of the most powerful of this class of models is the single hidden layer feedforward network. In such a network, the inputs x_i are associated with the outputs y_i through a matrix of weights that either magnify or attenuate the strength of the connection. The "hidden" units in the second layer process the sum of $x_i \alpha_{ij}$, $i = 1, \ldots, k$, by producing an activation according to the value of the threshold function $G(\alpha_j' X)$. Quite often, a logistic or sigmoid specification is chosen for the threshold specification.

A single hidden-layer, feedforward, neural network specification is

$$Y = F(X) = \sum_{j=1}^{K} \beta_j G(\alpha_j' X + \mu_j). \tag{6.2}$$

Here $G(u) = e^u/(1 + e^u)$ is the logistic distribution function; α_j is the vector of weights from each input x_i from the m-dimensional input vector X; and Y is an m-dimensional vector of outputs. The number of hidden units is indexed by k. Identification and estimation issues with regard to empirical implementation of (6.2) are discussed in Rummelhart, Hinton, and Williams (1986), Werbos (1974), and White (1989).

7. MODEL ORDER AND FORECAST ACCURACY

Tests involving forecast error and prediction error play a major role in the identification of time series models. We have seen how the concept of variance decomposition depends on the use of one-step-ahead forecasts. In selecting the lag order of a model, tests of final prediction error are employed; and in the application of time series models to forecasting, tests of forecast error are used to assess forecast accuracy.

Let us consider first the tests for lag order within a sample. It has been shown in UTM that the advantage of the likelihood ratio test stems from it being the only lag order test explicitly based on statistical distribution theory. However, deGooijer et al. (1985) and others have questioned its practicality in this context:

> The difficulties in determining the order of an ARMA model by using the Neyman-Pearson approach have introduced the important notion that one *should not* expect a finite number of observations on a time series process to give a clear cut answer about the true order of the process. (italics in original) (deGooijer et al., 1985, p. 312)

Clearly, one expects the same to hold true for VARMA models as well. As a result, other criteria are proposed that implicitly "test" for model order. These methods have adopted the concept of forecast error that evaluates the expected one-step-ahead prediction error of a pth order autoregressive process. Akaike (1969, 1970) was the first to propose such a test that balanced the errors associated with underestimation of the true order with the errors attributable to overestimation of the true order. This test is established through the use of a minimization criterion. In brief, the determination of model order p occurs when the value of the FPE ratio for a particular p is at a minimum or does not become lower as other orders of p are tested.

The measurement of forecast error plays an important role in identifying and testing a given multivariate or univariate time series model. Though testing for forecast accuracy is typically applied at a final model validation stage, these tests also can be helpful for model identification at an earlier stage. Most models explain a dependent time series variable adequately over a given sample period, but only a few properly specified models will predict the dependent variable adequately in the out-of-sample or forecast period. Evaluating forecast error thus provides a much more rigorous approach for testing the explanatory power or performance of a model.

TABLE 7.1

Criteria for Multivariate Model Order Selection

Name	Criterion	Measure	Critical Value
1. Likelihood Ratio (LR)			
	$p = \max\{LR(p) \mid p = 0, 1, \dots, L\}$	$LR(p) = T(\ln\mid\Sigma_{p-1}\mid - \ln\mid\Sigma_v\mid)$	$\chi^2 [m^2(v - k)]$
2. Final Prediction Error (FPE)			
	$p = \min\{FPE(p) \mid p = 0, 1, \dots, L\}$	$FPE(p) = \{(T + pm + 1)/(T - pm - 1)\}^m \mid\Sigma_p\mid$	N/A
3. Akaike Information Criterion (AIC)			
	$p = \min\{AIC(p) \mid p = 0, 1, \dots, L\}$	$AIC(p) = \ln\mid\Sigma_p\mid + \{(2m^2p)/T\}$	N/A
4. Bayesian Information Criterion (BIC)			
	$p = \min\{BIC(p) \mid p = 0, 1, \dots, L\}$	$BIC(p) = \ln\mid\Sigma_p\mid + \{(m^2p\ln T)/T\}$	N/A
5. Criterion Autoregressive Transfer Function (CAT)			
	$p = \min\{CAT(p) \mid p = 0, 1, \dots, L\}$		
	$CAT(p) = \text{trace}[m/T\Sigma_j\,(T\Sigma_j^*/T - jm + 1)^{-1} - (T\Sigma_p^*/T - pm - 1)^{-1}]$	for $j = 0, \dots, p$	
6. Shibata (S)			
	$p = \min\{S(p) \mid p = 0, 1, \dots, L\}$	$S(p) = \{1 + 2[(mp + 1)/T]\}^m \mid\Sigma_p\mid$	N/A
7. Hannan-Quinn (HQ1)			
	$p = \min\{HQ1(p) \mid p = 0, 1, \dots, L\}$	$HQ1(p) = \ln\mid\Sigma_p\mid + \{(2pm^2\ln\ln T)/T\}$	N/A
8. Hannan-Quinn (HQ2)			
	$p = \min\{HQ2(p) \mid p = 0, 1, \dots, L\}$	$HQ2(p) = \ln\mid\Sigma_p\mid + \{(2p\ln\ln T)/T\}$	N/A

NOTE: m is equal to the number of variables in the vector $X(t)$ and Σ_p is the variance-covariance matrix of the residuals for the multivariate specification.

Applications of tests of forecast accuracy to VAR models can be found in a number of sources, including Bessler and Kling (1986), Fackler and Krieger (1986), Kaylen (1988), and Lesage (1990a). N/A means none available.

Testing for Model Order

As was true in the univariate case, the selection of the number of lags to include in a multivariate time series model depends largely on the use of one or more minimization criteria, as listed in Table 7.1. Some of these criteria measure a model's explanatory power over the sample period, some over the forecast period, or a combination of both. Other attempts to determine model order are the approaches of Hsiao (1979), Kaylen (1988), and Tiao and Box (1981). Kaylen (1988) focuses on the method of exclusion of variables. This relaxes the assumption of symmetry within the system and tests explicitly for the number of lags associated with each variable in the system. In the case of asymmetry in the system, Kaylen suggests alternative estimation procedures. All of the above approaches would seem to be compatible with the Litterman (1986) Bayesian VAR procedures. Unfortunately, there is not a universal method for determining lag length; consequently, the practitioner must proceed with caution in using these criteria. For the sake of simplicity and convention, we recommend the multivariate extensions of the measures presented in UTM.

The principal difference between the univariate and multivariate cases depends on the method of defining the error variance measure component of the equations. In the multivariate case, the estimated error variance (i.e., σ_e^2) is replaced by the determinant of the error variance-covariance matrix (i.e., $|\Sigma|$) from the test equations. This change is necessary because in the multivariate case, the test equation(s) for the measures include lags of *both* $x(t)$ and $y(t)$, instead of only lags of the dependent variable (e.g., $x[t]$), which was the univariate case.

As an example, the Likelihood Ratio (LR) test is performed in the univariate case by using the following test equations, as presented in UTM

$$x(t) = \alpha_0 + \sum_{j=1}^{p-1} \alpha_j x(t-j) + e(t)$$

$$(7.1)$$

$$x(t) = \alpha_0 + \sum_{j=1}^{p} \alpha_j x(t-j) + v(t)$$

In the multivariate case, the test equations become

$$X(t) = \alpha_0 + \sum_{j=1}^{p-1} \alpha_j X(t-j) + e(t)$$

$$(7.2)$$

$$X(t) = \alpha_0 + \sum_{j=1}^{p} \alpha_j X(t-j) + v(t)$$

where $X(t-j)$ is a matrix of lagged independent variables including $x(t-j)$, for example, $X(t-j) = [x(t-j), y(t-j)]$. Note that the test equations for the other order criterion measures (e.g., FPE, AIC, etc.) are modified in a similar manner.

We need not discuss the order measures here in detail because a complete explanation appears in UTM. The interpretation and estimation issues relevant to each measure are also discussed in that work and apply as well to the multivariate case.

In terms of the choice of an order measure, Lutkepohl (1985) states that the Hannan-Quinn and Schwartz criterion both estimate the AR order k consistently, if $m \leq k$. The FPE, AIC, and the Shibata (1980) tests, although they are not consistent, overestimate p asymptotically with a positive probability, if $m > k$. Shibata (1980) has suggested that part of the overestimation problem can be solved by using his criterion rather than the AIC or FPE.

In conclusion, the researcher must be aware that the selection of a test criterion makes a difference in establishing model order. This result was illustrated by Cromwell and Hannan (1993), where it was shown that various model order results derived from the different order criteria presented above differed notably when applied to a regional economic data set. This should caution the reader that one's decision to use a particular test criterion should be based on some theoretical foundation (i.e., theories in the social sciences); or else several test criteria should be applied and the choice of one particular test defended.

Lastly, examination of the residuals from these order test equations may show that the condition of stationarity is violated. Once again, it is important to test for stationarity at the end as well as at the beginning of the lag selection procedure.

Testing for Forecast Accuracy

Forecast applications of time series models are not considered in this monograph. If anywhere, forecast applications and related tests should have been included in the first or univariate volume, UTM. Nevertheless, certain aspects of these tests are extremely important for understanding the full implications and properties of fitting time series models to economic and other social science data (e.g., see Labys & Pollak, 1984). In addition, a number of tests have recently appeared that are particularly appropriate for multivariate models.

In selecting a useful series of tests, we follow the goals suggested by Granger and Newbold (1986, p. 277):

TABLE 7.2
Tests Evaluating Forecast Accuracy

I. Accuracy of Individual Models

Parametric Tests	*Nonparametric Tests*
Coefficient tests	Single point criteria
Pseudo forecasts	(MAPE, MSE, RMSE)
Sensitivity analysis	Interval criteria
Direction and turning point analysis	Error-cost analysis
	Turning point analysis
	Sensitivity analysis

II. Comparative Accuracy Across Models

Parametric Tests

Granger-Newbold tests
Steckler test

1. How "good," in some sense, is a forecasting model or particular set of forecasts?
2. Is one forecasting model or a set of forecasts better than its competitors?

Several possible tests that have been proposed to evaluate those goals have been summarized in Table 7.2. The tests relate to the accuracy of a single time series model or to comparative accuracy across models. The tests have also been classified as to whether they are parametric or nonparametric.

Most of the tests presented so far to identify the various time series models have been parametric. That is, they require some form of normal, t, F, or other statistical distribution to perform hypothesis tests. Such distribution methods can be applied here to obtain further information as to how a time series model might perform in the out-of-sample period. Nonparametric tests constitute a variety of tests whose application does not depend on hypothesis tests based on a known statistical distribution. These tests are performed primarily in the out-of-sample period. Because the application of these tests is discussed in several sources (e.g., Labys & Pollack, 1984; Makridakis, 1984), we review them only briefly, concentrating instead on more recent developments.

Accuracy of Individual Models

Parametric Tests

Coefficient Tests. A traditional approach for evaluating forecast performance has been to determine the statistical properties of the regression coefficients in a given equation, where a particular functional form is assumed or given. Direct tests of these coefficients often meet with difficulty in time series models and instead one must apply goodness-of-fit tests, such as the coefficient of determination, the standard error of the estimate, and the chi-square or F statistics.

Pseudo Forecasts. Normally one has available a set of t observations on each of the independent and dependent variables of a model; however, some of these data can be "saved" for comparison purposes. Model estimation can thus be based on the shortened original series and forecast evaluation can be made by comparing the forecast values and the actual values of the "saved" series.

Sensitivity Analysis. It is also important to observe the sensitivity of equation solutions or forecasts to variations in the parameters of that equation. In the case of multivariate models, parameters of an independent variable can simply be varied systematically and variations in the solutions evaluated in terms of deviations from the base solution. F tests are often used to validate such response surfaces. In the case of the multivariate VAR models, such sensitivity analysis can also be performed by examining the responses in the impulse functions.

Direction and Turning Point Analysis. The Henriksson-Merton (1983) test, which evaluates the ability of the time-series model to predict directional changes in the forecast variable, meets the first goal set by Granger and Newbold. Merton proposes that if a forecast has any value, it must cause a rational observer to modify prior beliefs about the distribution of subsequent movements in the variable being forecast. Because of the complexity of such a test, Cumby and Modest (1987) suggest the following, simpler version. Let $\gamma_i(t) = 1$, if the forecast change for a particular series is nonnegative; otherwise $\gamma_i(t) = 0$. Under the null hypothesis that the forecast has no value, Henriksson and Merton showed that the following condition must hold

$$\text{Prob}[\gamma_i(t) = 0 \mid \Delta x_i(t) < 0] + \text{Prob}[\gamma_i(t) = 1 \mid \Delta x_i(t) \geq 0] = 1 \quad (7.3)$$

where $\Delta x_i(t)$ is the actual change in the ith variable of $x(t)$.

Test Procedure

Step 1. Let $x_i(t)$ be the actual value of the ith variable in the vector $x(t)$, and $\hat{x}_i(t)$ be the forecast value of $x_i(t)$.

Step 2. Perform the following regressions:

$$\Delta x_i(t) = \alpha_1 + \beta_1 z_i(t) + \varepsilon_1(t)$$

$$\Delta x_i(t) = \alpha_2 + \beta_2 \Delta \hat{x}_i(t) + \varepsilon_2(t)$$

where $z_i(t) = 1$ if $\Delta \hat{x}_i(t) > 0$ and $z_i(t) = 0$ if $\Delta \hat{x}_i(t) < 0$, and $\Delta \hat{x}_i(t) = \hat{x}_i(t) - \hat{x}_i(t-1)$.

Step 3. Form the null and alternative hypotheses.

H_0: Forecast has no value, $\beta_1 = 0$ or $\beta_2 = 0$
H_A: Forecast has value, $\beta_1 > 0$ or $\beta_2 > 0$

Step 4. Form the $t(\beta_i)$ statistic for the parameter β_i based on the regressions in Step 2.

Step 5. For a given significance level α, obtain the critical value τ from the student t distribution. Reject H_0 if the $|t_p| > |\tau|$.

The Henriksson-Merton test also can provide information about the number of times each model correctly and incorrectly predicts both upward and downward directional changes in the variables of interest. For a series of N observed out-of-sample forecasts for the variables, N_1 is the number of observations with positive revisions; N_2 is the number of observations with nonpositive revisions; total revisions are $N = N_1 + N_2$; n_1 is the number of successful predictions given a positive revision; n_2 is the number of unsuccessful predictions given a nonpositive revision; and the total is $n = n_1 + n_2$. One then tests to determine whether the observed number of successful predictions is unlikely under the null hypothesis of no forecasting ability. Let v represent the number of correct predictions. The null hypothesis of no forecasting ability is rejected when the probability of observing n_1 or more correct signs is unacceptably small. For a given significance level (α), the null hypothesis of no value in the forecasts is rejected when $n_1 \geq v^*$ is the solution to

$$\text{HM} = \sum_{v=v^*}^{n_1} \binom{N_1}{v} \binom{N_2}{n-v} \Bigg/ \binom{N}{n} = 1 - \alpha \qquad (7.4)$$

where n_1 is equal to the minimum of N_1 and n.

Test Procedure

Step 1. Obtain N out-of-sample forecasts for each variable. Define $N_1 =$ the number of positive changes, $N_2 =$ the number of negative changes, and $N = N_1 + N_2$.

Step 2. Count the number of successful predictions given positive changes n_1, and the number of successful predictions given negative changes n_2, where $n = n_1 + n_2$. Let v represent the number of correct predictions.

Step 3. Form the null and alternative hypotheses.

H_0: No forecast ability
H_A: Some forecast ability

Step 4. Choose v^* and form the test statistic (7.4) where $n_1 = \min(N_1, n)$.

Step 5. For a given significance level α, reject H_O if HM $= 1 - \alpha$.

Nonparametric Tests

Single Point Criteria. The most popular tests that have been traditionally applied to measure the forecast error between actual and forecast observations are single point criteria, such as the mean absolute percentage error, the mean squared error, and the root mean squared error.

$$\text{MAPE} = \frac{1}{T} \sum_{t=1}^{T} \frac{|x(t) - x^*(t)|}{x(t)} \cdot 100 \tag{7.5}$$

$$\text{MSE} = \frac{1}{T} \sum_{t=1}^{T} [x(t) - x^*(t)]^2 \tag{7.6}$$

$$\text{RMSE} = \left[\frac{1}{T} \sum_{t=1}^{T} [x(t) - x^*(t)]^2 \right]^{\frac{1}{2}} \tag{7.7}$$

Here $x(t)$ = actual observation values and $x^*(t)$ = forecast or estimated values in the out-of-sample period, $t = 1, 1, \ldots, T$. These tests can also be made in the context of the "pseudo forecasts" discussed earlier.

Although the error criteria relate to period-by-period error, they can also be applied to the analysis of multiperiod forecast analysis. Little, however, is presently known about the use of multiperiod forecast error to compare the validity of alternative models.

Interval Criteria. If the modeler is more interested in predicting an interval or range of values, then a test of confidence intervals can be developed and applied for this purpose.

Error-Cost Analysis. Although the above criteria probably are the most practical for evaluating performance with a historical sample or a small post-sample data set, they fail to define the surrounding probabilistic conditions in a way that would be useful with a large post-sample data set. There are two ways to improve this situation. First, an informative forecast could accompany the point forecasts based on some mathematical statement regarding the probability distributions surrounding these forecasts. This amounts to an interval forecast in which the point forecast is now presented along with an appropriate confidence interval. Second, a decision forecast could be prepared that recommends that the forecast be accepted in relation to some alternative consequence.

For example, Granger and Newbold (1986) consider the case where the policy maker must decide on a certain policy that depends upon the future value $x^*(t)$ of a dependent variable $x(t)$. The future value, of course, is not known and the policy maker could make an incorrect decision. The loss or consequence the policy maker must undergo in such a case is given by the loss function $L[D_i, x(t)]$, which describes the loss of selecting decision D_i when $x(t)$ turns out to be the true value of $x^*(t)$.

Turning Point Analysis. A major characterization of a model's performance is its ability to explain the turning points of fluctuations in values of a dependent variable. There are a number of descriptive variables or statistics that can be used to evaluate turning point errors. Most often they pertain to the number of turning points missed, the number of turning points falsely predicted, the number of under- and over-predictions, rank correlations of predicted and actual changes, and various tests of randomness in prediction. Naik and Leuthold (1986) have suggested a method of evaluating turning-point performance based on the use of contingency tables. Henriksson and Merton (1983) also provide a parameter test, as described earlier.

Comparative Accuracy Across Models

Validation also can take the form of comparing the forecast errors derived from a multivariate time series model to the errors obtained, for example, from a univariate model, an econometric model, or even judgmental methods. This comparative approach has been demonstrated by Granger (1990), Granger and Newbold (1986), Labys and Granger (1970), Mahmoud (1984), Makridakis (1984), Park (1990), and Skaggs and Snyder (1992). Granger and Newbold, in particular, indicate that the forecast errors derived from two different models or generating mechanisms cannot be compared simply by using the variance ratio or F test. The errors generated by one mechanism may be correlated with those produced by another. And for forecasts of more than one step ahead, the errors may not be white noise even for optimal forecasts. Below, we present their proposed test as an alternative.

Granger-Newbold Test. Consider the forecast errors generated from two different models.

$$e_1(t) = x_1(t) - x_1^*(t) \quad \text{from Model 1}$$

$$(7.8)$$

$$e_2(t) = x_2(t) - x_2^*(t) \quad \text{from Model 2}$$

Assume that $e_1(t)$ and $e_2(t)$ constitute a random sample from a bivariate normal distribution with means zero, variances σ_1^2 and σ_2^2 and correlation coefficient p.

$$E[e_1(t)] = E[e_2(t)] = 0$$

In this case the individual forecasts are unbiased and the forecast errors noncorrelated.

Form a pair of random variables given by $e_1(t) + e_2(t)$ and $e_1(t) - e_2(t)$. In this case

$$E\{[e_1(t) + e_2(t)][e_1(t) - e_2(t)]\} = \sigma_1^2 - \sigma_2^2 . \tag{7.9}$$

Given the assumption of unbiasedness, the two error variances and the two expected square errors will be equal if and only if this pair of random variables is uncorrelated. The test Granger and Newbold propose to evaluate zero correlations is based on the sample correlation coefficient

$$r = \frac{\displaystyle\sum_{t=1}^{T} [e_1(t) + e_2(t)][e_1(t) - e_2(t)]}{\left[\displaystyle\sum_{t=1}^{T} [e_1(t) + e_2(t)]^2 \sum_{t=1}^{T} [e_1(t) - e_2(t)]^2 \right]^{\frac{1}{2}}} . \tag{7.10}$$

This coefficient is then used to form a test statistic that compares the equality of the (expected) squared forecast errors from each model.

$$Z = [\ln(1 + r) - \ln(1 - r)] \frac{(T-3)^{\frac{1}{2}}}{2} \tag{7.11}$$

where r is the sample correlation obtained from (7.10) and T is the number of out-of-sample predictions. Under the null hypothesis of no correlation, Z is approximately distributed $N(0,1)$.

Test Procedure

Step 1. Obtain the forecast errors, $e_1(t)$ and $e_2(t)$, from two competing models, Model 1 and Model 2.

Step 2. Form the null and alternative hypotheses.

Step 3. Form the test statistic

$$Z = [\ln(1 + r) - \ln(1 - r)](T - 3)^{\frac{1}{2}}/2$$

where *r* is the correlation coefficient from (7.10).

Step 4. For a given significance level α, obtain the critical value z from the standard normal distribution. Reject H_0 if $|Z| > |z|$.

Steckler Test. Another approach compares the accuracy of forecasts generated by different models employing a ranking procedure. In this case, each model is ranked according to its forecast accuracy, the latter being measured by the root mean squared error. A score equal to the ranking is assigned to each forecasting model. If several variables are being forecast, as in the multivariate case, then a score equal to the ranking is assigned to each variable. Aggregate scores are obtained for each of the series by summing the rankings across the given forecast horizon.

If the time series models have equal forecast accuracy, the scores would have the same expected value for each model. A χ^2 goodness-of-fit statistic is used to test for differences in forecast accuracy by examining whether the aggregate score differs significantly from the expected score, assuming the models had equal forecast accuracy. This criterion explicitly compares the complete set of forecasts over each period for each model.

8. COMPUTATIONAL METHODS
FOR PERFORMING THE TESTS

The purpose of this chapter is to provide some insights into the software available for constructing the models and performing the tests proposed here. To better facilitate this endeavor, we suggest software such as MicroTSP (1992), RATS, and SHAZAM, which can perform some of the identification tests and the estimation of the regression models associated with each chapter. In Table 8.1, a classification has been provided as to which software can best perform a particular test of interest.

Clearly, very few tests are explicitly included in these software packages—or others for that matter. Tests of normality and the Portmanteau test

TABLE 8.1

Microcomputer Software for Performing Time Series Tests

Test	MICROTSP[a]	RATS[b]	SHAZAM[c]
Fountis-Dickey	N	V	V
Skewness	N	V	V
Kurtosis	N	V	V
Multivariate Portmanteau	N	V	V
CRDW	V	V	V
DF	Y	Y	Y
ADF	Y	Y	Y
Engle-Granger	V	V	V
Johansen	N	V	Y
Granger-Lee	V	V	V
Granger	Y	Y	V
Sims	V	Y	V
Pierce-Haugh	V	V	V
Geweke	V	V	V
VAR(M)	Y	Y	Y
VMA(M)	N	Y	N
BVAR(M)	N	Y	V
VARMA(M)	N	Y	N
ECM(M)	V	V	V
Impulse Response	Y	Y	V
Variance Decompositions	Y	Y	V
Neural Networks	N	N	N
Likelihood Ratio	V	V	V
FPE	V	V	V
CAT	V	V	V
AIC	V	V	V
BIC	V	V	V
BEC	V	V	V
S	V	V	V
HQ	V	V	V
MAPE	Y	Y	Y
MSE	Y	Y	Y
RMSE	Y	Y	Y
Granger-Newbold	V	V	V
Henriksson-Merton 1	V	V	V
Henriksson-Merton 2	V	V	V

NOTES: Y stands for a feature of the package. V suggests that the estimation can be performed but the test is not a feature in the software package. The test can be done, however, with auxiliary work outside the package. N means that the test cannot be performed with the package. M implies that model estimation can be performed.

a. MicroTSP, Quantitative Micro Software, 4521 Campus Drive, Suite 336, Irvine, CA 92715.

b. RATS, VAR Econometrics, 134 Prospect Avenue So., Minneapolis, MN 55419.

c. SHAZAM, UBC Economics, No. 997-1873 East Mall, Vancouver, BC, V6T-1Z1, Canada.

for independence as presented here can only be performed using the matrix algebra of the RATS and SHAZAM packages. The Fountis-Dickey test can only be computed using software that provides eigenvalue and eigenvector computation. Again this refers to SHAZAM and RATS. MicroTSP has versions of the Dickey-Fuller and Augmented Dickey-Fuller tests for evaluating cointegration, but it does not have the CRDW or the Engle-Granger tests. Although MicroTSP also has the Granger causality test, it excludes the Sims, Geweke, and Pierce-Haugh tests. RATS has a routine for the Granger and Sims tests but not the Geweke and Pierce-Haugh procedures. SHAZAM and RATS provide environments for performing these tests but not without programming efforts on the part of the user.

Model estimation for transfer function models can easily be accomplished in all three packages, but MicroTSP provides the easiest procedures for estimating VAR models, impulse responses, and variance decompositions. RATS can perform BVAR along with confidence interval estimation for impulse responses. None of the packages have routines for ECM or VARMA modeling; ECM modeling, however, can be done using all three packages.

These packages also provide forecast statistics such as MAPE, MSE, and RMSE, but they do not include the Granger-Newbold and different forms of the Henriksson-Merton tests. Related test information can be found in a review of appropriate forecast software by Beaumont, Mahmoud, and McGee (1985). None of the packages provide statistics for model order determination measures, although RATS and SHAZAM can perform this function with a user written routine. Because of the matrix algebra involved, MicroTSP cannot perform this function.

Overall, MicroTSP provides an efficient vehicle for performing many of the basic multivariate tests. One must, however, turn to other software to perform the more difficult tests proposed here and in UTM. Both SHAZAM and RATS have features that make them attractive for supplementing the MicroTSP package. Writing the routines for utilizing the above mentioned tests, however, could prove to be somewhat intractable for many researchers.

APPENDIX
Statistical Tables

TABLE A.1
Critical Values for the Dickey-Fuller Test

Sample Size T	Significance Level							
	0.01	0.025	0.05	0.10	0.90	0.95	0.975	0.99
No Constant Included in (2.1), τ_1								
25	−2.66	−2.26	−1.95	−1.60	0.92	1.33	1.70	2.16
50	−2.62	−2.25	−1.95	−1.61	0.91	1.31	1.66	2.08
100	−2.60	−2.24	−1.95	−1.61	0.90	1.29	1.64	2.03
250	−2.58	−2.23	−1.95	−1.62	0.89	1.29	1.63	2.01
300	−2.58	−2.23	−1.95	−1.62	0.89	1.28	1.62	2.00
∞	−2.58	−2.23	−1.95	−1.62	0.89	1.28	1.62	2.00
Constant Included in (2.1), τ_2								
25	−3.75	−3.33	−3.00	−2.62	−0.37	0.00	0.34	0.72
50	−3.58	−3.22	−2.93	−2.60	−0.40	−0.03	0.29	0.66
100	−3.51	−3.17	−2.89	−2.58	−0.42	−0.05	0.26	0.63
250	−3.46	−3.14	−2.88	−2.57	−0.42	−0.06	0.24	0.62
300	−3.44	−3.13	−2.87	−2.57	−0.43	−0.07	0.24	0.61
∞	−3.43	−3.12	−2.86	−2.57	−0.44	−0.07	0.23	0.60
Constant and Linear Trend Included in (2.1), τ_3								
25	−4.38	−3.95	−3.60	−3.24	−1.14	−0.80	−0.50	−0.15
50	−4.15	−3.80	−3.50	−3.18	−1.19	−0.87	−0.58	−0.24
100	−4.04	−3.73	−3.45	−3.15	−1.22	−0.90	−0.62	−0.28
250	−3.99	−3.69	−3.43	−3.13	−1.23	−0.92	−0.64	−0.31
300	−3.98	−3.68	−3.42	−3.13	−1.24	−0.93	−0.65	−0.32
∞	−3.96	−3.66	−3.41	−3.12	−1.25	−0.94	−0.66	−0.33

NOTE: This table was constructed by David A. Dickey using Monte Carlo methods. Standard errors of the estimates vary, but most are less than 0.02. The table is reproduced from Fuller (1976). Copyright © Wayne A. Fuller, *An Introduction to Time Series Analyses,* John Wiley & Sons, Inc., 1976. Reprinted by permission of John Wiley and Sons, Inc.

TABLE A.2
Critical Values and Power of the Engle-Granger Test

Model I: $\Delta y, \Delta x$ *independent standard normal, 100 observations, 10,000 replications, p = 4.*

Statistic	Critical Values			
	Name	1%	5%	10%
1	CRDW	0.51	0.39	0.32
2	DF	4.07	3.37	3.03
3	ADF	3.77	3.17	2.84
4	RVAR	18.3	13.6	11.0
5	ARVAR	15.8	11.8	9.7
6	UVAR	23.4	18.6	16.0
7	AUVAR	22.6	17.9	15.5

Model II: $y_t + 2x_t = u_t, \Delta u_t = (\rho - 1)u_{t-1} + \varepsilon_t, x_t + y_t = v_t, \Delta v_t = \eta_t,$ $\rho = .8, .9, 100$ *observations, 1,000 replications, p = 4.*

Statistic	Rejections per 100: $\rho = .9$			
	Name	1%	5%	10%
1	CRDW	4.8	19.9	33.6
2	DF	2.2	15.4	29.0
3	ADF	1.5	11.0	22.7
4	RVAR	2.3	11.4	25.3
5	ARVAR	1.0	9.2	17.9
6	UVAR	4.3	13.3	26.1
7	AUVAR	1.6	8.3	16.3

Statistic	Rejections per 100: $\rho = .8$			
	Name	1%	5%	10%
1	CRDW	34.0	66.4	82.1
2	DF	20.5	59.2	76.1
3	ADF	7.8	30.9	51.6
4	RVAR	15.8	46.2	67.4
5	ARVAR	4.6	22.4	39.0
6	UVAR	19.0	45.9	63.7
7	AUVAR	4.8	18.3	33.4

TABLE A.2

(continued)

Model I: $\Delta y_t = .8\Delta y_{t-4} + \varepsilon_t$, $\Delta x_t = .8\Delta x_{t-4} + \eta_t$; *100 observations, 10,000 replications,*
$p = 4$, ε_t, η_t, *independent standard normal.*

Statistic	Critical Values			
	Name	1%	5%	10%
1	CRDW	0.46	0.28	0.21
2	DF	3.90	3.05	2.71
3	ADF	3.73	3.17	2.91
4	RVAR	37.2	22.4	17.2
5	ARVAR	16.2	12.3	10.5
6	UVAR	59.0	40.3	31.3
7	AUVAR	28.0	22.0	19.2

Model II: $y_t + 2x_t = u_t$, $\Delta u_t = (\rho - 1)u_{t-1} + .8\Delta u_{t-4} + \varepsilon_t$, $y_t + x_t = v_t$, $\Delta v_t = .8\Delta v_{t-4} + \eta_t$;
$\rho = .9, .8$. *100 observations, 1,000 replications, p = 4.*

Statistic	Rejections per 100: $\rho = .9$			
	Name	1%	5%	10%
1	CRDW	15.6	39.9	65.6
2	DF	9.4	25.5	37.8
3	ADF	36.0	61.2	72.2
4	RVAR	.3	4.4	10.9
5	ARVAR	26.4	48.5	62.8
6	UVAR	.0	.5	3.5
7	AUVAR	9.4	26.8	40.3

Statistic	Rejections per 100: $\rho = .8$			
	Name	1%	5%	10%
1	CRDW	77.5	96.4	98.6
2	DF	66.8	89.7	96.0
3	ADF	68.9	90.3	94.4
4	RVAR	7.0	42.4	62.5
5	ARVAR	57.2	80.5	89.3
6	UVAR	2.5	10.8	25.9
7	AUVAR	32.2	53.0	67.7

SOURCE: From "Co-integration and Error Correction: Representation Estimation and Testing" by R. F. Engle and C. W. J. Granger, 1987, *Econometrica, 55*, pp. 251-276. Copyright © 1986 by *Econometrica*. Reprinted by permission.

TABLE A.3
Critical Values for the Engle-Yoo Cointegration Test

Number of Var's N	Sample Size T	Significance Level		
		1%	5%	10%
1[a]	50	2.62	1.95	1.61
	100	2.60	1.95	1.61
	250	2.58	1.95	1.62
	500	2.58	1.95	1.62
	∞	2.58	1.95	1.62
1[b]	50	3.58	2.93	2.60
	100	3.51	2.89	2.58
	250	3.46	2.88	2.57
	500	3.44	2.87	2.57
	∞	3.43	2.86	2.57
2	50	4.32	3.67	3.28
	100	4.07	3.37	3.03
	200	4.00	3.37	3.02
3	50	4.84	4.11	3.73
	100	4.45	3.93	3.59
	200	4.35	3.78	3.47
4	50	4.94	4.35	4.02
	100	4.75	4.22	3.89
	200	4.70	4.18	3.89
5	50	5.41	4.76	4.42
	100	5.18	4.58	4.26
	200	5.02	4.48	4.18

SOURCE: From "Forecasting and Testing in Cointegrated Systems" by R. F. Engle and B. S. Yoo, 1987, *Journal of Econometrics, 35,* pp. 143-159. Copyright © 1987 by *Journal of Econometrics.* Reprinted by permission.
NOTES: a. Critical values of $\hat{\tau}$.
b. Critical values of $\hat{\tau}_\mu$. Both cited from Fuller (1976, p. 373).

REFERENCES

AKAIKE, H. (1969) "Fitting autoregressions for prediction." *Annals of the Institute of Statistical Mathematics* 21: 243-247.

AKAIKE, H. (1970) "Autoregressive model fitting for control." *Annals of the Institute of Statistical Mathematics* 22: 163-180.

ANDERSON, T. W. (1958) *An Introduction to Multivariate Statistical Analysis.* New York: John Wiley.

ANDREWS, D. F., GNANADESIKAN, R., and WARNER, J. L. (1971) "Transformations of multivariate data." *Biometrika* 27: 825-840.

ASHLEY, T., GRANGER, C. W. J., and SCHMALENSEE, R. (1980) "Advertising and aggregate consumption: An analysis of causality." *Econometrica* 48: 1149-1167.

BAEK, E. G., and BROCK, W. A. (1988) *A Nonparametric test for temporal dependence in a vector time series.* Unpublished manuscript, University of Wisconsin, Madison.

BANNERJEE, A., DOLADO, J., GALBRAITH, J. W., and HENRY, D. F. (1993) *Cointegration, Error Correction, and the Econometric Analysis of Non-stationary Data.* Oxford: Oxford University Press.

BEAUMONT, C., MAHMOUD, E., and McGEE, V. E. (1985) "Microcomputer forecasting software: A survey." *Journal of Forecasting* 4: 305-312.

BESSLER, D. A., and KLING, J. L. (1986) "Forecasting vector autoregressions with Bayesian priors." *American Journal of Agricultural Economics* 68: 144-151.

BOX, G. E. P., and JENKINS, G. M. (1976) *Time Series Analysis: Forecasting and Control.* Revised edition. San Francisco: Holden-Day.

BROCK, W. A., DECHERT, W., and SCHEINKMAN, J. (1986) "A test of independence based on the correlation dimension." SSRI Report #8702, Department of Economics, University of Wisconsin, University of Houston, and University of Chicago.

CAINES, P. E., KENG, C. W., and SETHI, S. P. (1981) "Causality analysis and multivariate autoregressive modeling with an application to supermarket sales analysis." *Journal of Economic Dynamics and Control* 3: 267-298.

CARGILL, T. F., and MORUS, S. A. (1988) "A vector autoregression model for the Nevada economy." *Economic Review Federal Reserve Bank of San Francisco,* Winter: 21-32.

CHAMBERLAIN, G. (1982) "The general equivalence of Granger and Sims causality." *Econometrica* 50: 569-581.

CHITTURI, R. V. (1974) "Distribution of residual autocorrelations in multiple autoregressive schemes." *Journal of the American Statistical Association* 69: 928-934.

COOLEY, J. F., and PRESCOTT, E. C. (1973) "Varying parameter regression: A theory and some applications." *Annals of Economic and Social Measurements* 463-473.

CORMAN, H., JOYCE, T., and LOVITCH, N. (1987) "Crime, deterrence and the business cycle in New York City: A VAR approach." *Review of Economics and Statistics* 69: 696-700.

CROMWELL, J. B., and HANNAN, M. J. (1988) "Regional Econometric Modeling Using Bayesian Vector Autoregressive Techniques: The Case of West Virginia." Working Paper, Regional Research Institute, West Virginia University, Morgantown, WV.

CROMWELL, J. B., and HANNAN, M. J. (1993) "The utility of impulse response functions in regional analysis: Some critical issues." *International Regional Science Review* 15: 199-222.

CROMWELL, J. B., LABYS, W. C., and TERRAZA, M. (1994) *Univariate Tests for Time Series Models.* Sage University Paper series on Quantitative Applications in the Social Sciences, 07-099. Thousand Oaks, CA: Sage.

CUMBY, R. E., and MODEST, D. M. (1987) "Testing for market timing ability: A framework for forecast evaluation." *Journal of Financial Economics* 19: 169-190.

DeGOOIJER, J. G., ABRAHAM, B., GOULD, A., and ROBINSON, L. (1985) "Methods for determining the order of an autoregressive-moving average process: A survey." *International Statistical Review* 53: 301-329.

DICKEY, D. A., and FULLER, W. A. (1979) "Distribution of the estimators for autoregressive time series with a unit root." *Journal of the American Statistical Association* 74: 427-431.

DOAN, T. A. (1988) *User's Manual: RATS Version 3.00.* Evanston, IL: VAR Econometrics, Inc.

DOAN, T. A., LITTERMAN, R. B., and SIMS, C. A. (1984) "Forecasting and conditional projections using realistic prior distributions." *Econometric Reviews* 3: 1-100.

EFRON, B. (1982) *The Jacknife, the Bootstrap and Other Resampling Plans.* Philadelphia: Society for Industrial and Applied Mathematics.

ENGLE, R. F., and GRANGER, C. W. J. (1987) "Co-integration and error correction: Representation, estimation and testing." *Econometrica* 55: 251-276.

ENGLE, R. F., and GRANGER, C. W. J. (1991) *Long-Run Economic Relationships.* Oxford: Oxford University Press.

ENGLE, R. F., HENDRY, D. F., and RICHARD, J. F. (1983) "Exogeneity." *Econometrica* 51: 277-304.

ENGLE, R. F., and YOO, B. F. (1987) "Forecasting and testing in co-integrated systems." *Journal of Econometrics* 35: 143-159.

FACKLER, J. S., and KRIEGER, S. G. (1986) "An application of vector time series techniques to macroeconomic forecasting." *Journal of Business and Economic Statistics* 4: 71-80.

FEIGE, E. L., and PEARCE, D. K. (1979) "The causal relationship between money and income: Some caveats for time series analysis." *Review of Economics and Statistics* 61: 521-533.

FOMBY, T. B., and RHODES, G. R. (1990) *Cointegration, Spurious Regressions and Unit Roots.* Greenwich, CT: JAI Press.

FOUNTIS, N. G., and DICKEY, D. A. (1989) "Testing for a unit root stationarity in multivariate autoregressive time series." *The Annals of Statistics* 17: 419-428.

FULLER, W. A. (1976) *An Introduction to Statistical Time Series.* New York: John Wiley.

GEWEKE, J. (1982) "Measurement of linear dependence and feedback between time series." *Journal of the American Statistical Association* 77: 304-324.

GEWEKE, J. (1984) "Inference and causality in economic time series models," in Z. Griliches and M. D. Intriligator (eds.), *Handbook of Econometrics* (Vol. 2, pp. 1101-1144). Amsterdam: North-Holland.

GEWEKE, J., MEESE, R., and DENT, W. (1983) "Comparing alternative tests of causality in temporal systems: Analytic results and experimental evidence." *Journal of Econometrics* 21: 161-194.

GRANGER, C. W. J. (1969) "Investigating causal relations by econometric models and cross-spectral methods." *Econometrica* 37: 424-438.

GRANGER, C. W. J. (1981) "Some properties of time series data and their use in econometric model specification." *Journal of Econometrics* 35: 143-159.

GRANGER, C. W. J. (1986) "Developments in the study of cointegrated economic variables." *Oxford Bulletin of Economics and Statistics* 48: 213-229.

GRANGER, C. W. J. (1987a) "Causality, cointegration and control." Working Paper, Department of Economics, University of California, San Diego.

GRANGER, C. W. J. (1987b) "Causality testing of control variables." Economics Department Discussion Paper, University of California, San Diego.

GRANGER, C. W. J. (ed.) (1990) *Modelling Economic Series: Readings in Econometric Methodology.* Oxford: Oxford University Press.

GRANGER, C. W. J., and ANDERSEN, A. P. (1978) *An Introduction to Bilinear Time Series Models.* Gottingen, The Netherlands: Vandenhoek & Ruprechet.

GRANGER, C. W. J., and LEE, T. H. (1989) "Investigation of production, sales and inventory relationships using multicointegration and nonsymmetric error correction models." *Journal of Applied Econometrics* 4: 5145-5159.

GRANGER, C. W. J., and LEE, T. H. (1990) "Multicointegration," in G. F. Rhodes Jr. and T. B. Fomby (eds.), *Advances in Econometrics* (pp. 71-84). Greenwich, CT: JAI Press.

GRANGER, C. W. J., and NEWBOLD, P. (1986) *Forecasting Economic Time Series* (2nd ed.). New York: Academic Press.

GRUBEN, W. C., and LONG, W. T. (1988) "Forecasting the Texas economy: Applications and evaluation of a systematic multivariate time series model." *Economic Review* Federal Reserve Bank of Dallas, Spring: 11-28.

HALL, S. G. (1986) "An application of the Granger-Engle two step procedure to United Kingdom aggregate wage data." *Oxford Bulletin of Economics and Statistics* 48: 229-239.

HANNAN, E. J. (1970) *Multiple Time Series.* New York: John Wiley.

HARVEY, A. C. (1990) *Forecasting, Structural Time Series Models and the Kalman Filter.* Cambridge: Cambridge University Press.

HAUGH, L. D. (1976) "Checking the independence of two covariance-stationary time series: A univariate residual cross-correlation approach." *Journal of the American Statistical Association* 71: 378-385.

HENRIKSSON, R. D., and MERTON, R. C. (1981) "Market timing and mutual fund performance: An empirical investigation." *Journal of Business* 57: 73-96.

HOEHN, J. G., GRUBEN, W. C., and FOMBY, T. B. (1984) "Time series forecasting models of the Texas economy: A comparison." *Economic Review, Federal Reserve Bank of Dallas,* May: 11-23.

HOSKING, J. R. M. (1981) "Lagrange multiplier tests of multivariate time series models." *Journal of The Royal Statistical Society* Series B, 43: 219-230.

HSIAO, C. (1979) "Causality tests in econometrics." *Journal of Economic Dynamics and Control* 1: 321-346.

JOHANSEN, S. (1988) "Statistical analysis of co-integration vectors." *Journal of Economic Dynamics and Control* 12: 231-254.

JUDGE, G. G., GRIFFITHS, W. E., CARTER HILL, R., LUTKEPOHL, H., and LEE, T.-C. (1985) *The Theory and Practice of Econometrics*. New York: John Wiley.

KALMAN, R. E. (1960) "A new approach to linear filtering and prediction problems." *Journal of Basic Engineering* 82: 34-45.

KANG, H. (1981) "Necessary and sufficient conditions for causality testing in multivariate ARMA models." *Journal of Time Series Analysis* 2: 95-101.

KANG, H. (1985) "The effects of detrending in Granger causality tests." *Journal of Business and Economic Statistics* 3: 344-349.

KANG, H. (1989) "The optimal lag selection and transfer function analysis in Granger causality tests." *Journal of Economic Dynamics and Control* 13: 151-169.

KAYLEN, M. S. (1988) "Vector autoregression forecasting models: Recent developments applied to the U.S. hog market." *American Journal of Agricultural Economics* 3: 701-712.

KLOEK, T., and VAN DIJK, H. K. (1978) "Bayesian estimates of equation system parameters: An application of integration by Monte Carlo." *Econometrica* 46: 1-20.

LABYS, W. C., and GRANGER, C. W. J. (1970) *Speculation, Hedging and Commodity Price Forecasts*. Lexington, MA: Heath Lexington.

LABYS, W. C., and LORD, M. (1992) "Inventory and equilibrium adjustments in international commodity markets: A multi-cointegration approach." *Applied Economics* 23: 1-8.

LABYS, W. C., and MAIZELS, A. (1993) "Commodity price fluctuations and macroeconomic adjustment in the developed economies." *Journal of Policy Modeling* 15: 335-352.

LABYS, W. C., MURCIA, V., and TERRAZA, M. (1994) "Modeling the petroleum spot market: A vector autoregressive approach," in J. Percebois and J. B. Lesourd (eds.), *Models for Energy Policy*. London: Chapman Hall.

LABYS, W. C., NAKKAR, N., and TERRAZA, M. (1993) "Modelisation Espace D'Etats des Marches des Products du Base." Working Paper, CEPE-LAMTA, University of Montpellier.

LABYS, W. C., and POLLAK, P. (1984) *Commodity Models for Forecasting and Policy Analysis*. London: Croom-Helm.

LESAGE, J. P. (1990a) "A comparison of forecasting ability of ECM and VAR models." *Review of Economics and Statistics* 72: 664-671.

LESAGE, J. P. (1990b) "Forecasting metropolitan employment using an export base error correction model." *Journal of Regional Science* 30: 307-323.

LITTERMAN, R. B. (1984) "Forecasting and policy analysis with Bayesian vector autoregression models." *Quarterly Review, Federal Reserve Bank of Minneapolis*, Fall: 30-41.

LITTERMAN, R. B. (1986) "Forecasting with Bayesian vector autoregressions—Five years of experience." *Journal of Business and Economic Statistics* 4: 25-38.

LUTKEPOHL, H. (1982) "Differencing multiple time series: Another look at Canadian money and income data." *Journal of Time Series Analysis* 3: 235-243.

LUTKEPOHL, H. (1985) "Comparison of criteria for estimating the order of a vector autoregressive process." *Journal of Time Series Analysis* 6: 35-52.

LUTKEPOHL, H. (1989) "A note on the asymptotic distribution of impulse response functions of estimated VAR models with orthogonal residuals." *Journal of Econometrics* 42: 371-376.

LUTKEPOHL, H. (1990) "Asymptotic distributions of impulse responses and forecast error variance decompositions of vector autoregressive models." *Review of Economics and Statistics* 72: 106-126.

MacKUEN, M., ERIKSON, R. S., and STIMSON, J. A. (1992) "Moving attractors and character of partisan change." *American Political Science Review* 86: 100-110.

MAGE, D. T. (1982) "An objective graphical method for testing normal distributed assumptions using probability plots." *American Statistician* 36: 116-120.

MAHMOUD, E. (1984) "Accuracy in forecasting: A survey." *Journal of Forecasting* 3: 139-159.

MAKRIDAKIS, S. (1984) *The Accuracy of Time Series Forecasting Methods.* London: John Wiley.

MARDIA, K. V. (1970) "Measures of multivariate skewness and kurtosis with applications." *Biometrika* 57: 519-520.

McKINNON, J. G. (1990) "Critical values for co-integration tests." Working Paper, University of California, San Diego.

MicroTSP 7.0. (1992) Quantitative Micro Software. Irvine, CA.

MILLS, T. C. (1990) *Time Series Techniques for Economists.* Cambridge: Cambridge University Press.

NACHANE, D. M., NADKARNI, R. M., and KARNIK, A. V. (1988) "Co-integration and causality testing of the energy-GDP relationship: A cross-country study." *Applied Economics* 20: 1511-1531.

NAIK, G., and LEUTHOLD, R. M. (1986) "A note on qualitative forecast evaluation." *American Journal of Agricultural Economics* 68: 721-726.

PARK, T. (1990) "Forecast evaluation for multivariate time series models." *Western Journal of Agricultural Economics* 15: 133-143.

PIERCE, D. A., and HAUGH, L. D. (1977) "Causality in temporal systems: Characterizations and a survey." *Journal of Econometrics* 5: 265-293.

PINDYCK, R. S., and RUBINFELD, D. L. (1976) *Econometric Models and Economic Forecasts.* New York: McGraw-Hill.

QUENOUILLE, M. H. (1957) *The Analysis of Multiple Time Series.* London: Griffin.

RATS, 3.0. VAR Econometrics, Minneapolis, MN.

RIISE, T., and TJOSTHEIM, D. (1985) "Theory and practice of multivariate ARMA forecasting." *Journal of Forecasting* 3: 309-317.

RUMELHART, D. E., HINTON, G. E., and WILLIAMS, R. J. (1986) "Learning internal representations by error propagation," in D. E. Rumelhart and J. L. McClelland (eds.), *Parallel Distributed Processing: Exploration in the Micro Structure of Cognition* (Vol. 1, pp. 318-362). Cambridge: MIT Press.

RUNKLE, D. (1987) "Vector autoregressions and reality." *Journal of Business and Economic Statistics* 5: 437-449.

SAS. (1985) *SAS User's Guide: Basics, Version 5.* Cary, NC: SAS Institute.

SEBER, G. A. F. (1984) *Multivariate Observations.* New York: John Wiley.

SHAZAM. (n.d.) *User's Reference Manual.* Version 6.2. New York: McGraw-Hill.

SHIBATA, R. (1980) "Asymptotically efficient selection of the order of the model for estimating parameters of a linear process." *The Annals of Statistics* 8: 147-164.

SIMS, C. A. (1972) "Money, income and causality." *American Economic Review* 62: 540-552.

SIMS, C. A. (1981) "Macroeconomics and reality." *Econometrica* 48: 1-48.

SKAGGS, R. K., and SNYDER, D. L. (1992) "A comparison of selected methods for forecasting monthly alfalfa hay prices." *Agribusiness* 8: 309-321.

SPSSx. (1983) *SPSSx User's Guide*. Chicago: SPSS Inc./McGraw-Hill.

STIMSON, J. A. (1991) *Public Opinion in America: Moods, Cycles and Swings*. Boulder, CO: Westview.

SUBBA RAO, T. (1981) "On the theory of bilinear time series models." *Journal of Royal Statistical Society B* 43: 244-255.

TIAO, G. C., and BOX, G. E. P. (1981) "Modeling multiple time series with applications." *Journal of the American Statistical Association* 76: 802-816.

WERBOS, P. J. (1974) "Beyond regression: New tools for prediction and analysis in the behavioral sciences." Master's thesis, Harvard University.

WHITE, H. (1989) "Some asymptotic results for learning in single hidden-layer feedback network models." *Journal of the American Statistical Association* 84: 1003-1013.

ZELLNER, A. (1979) "Causality and econometrics," in K. Brunner and A. Meltzer (eds.), *Carnegie-Rochester Conference Series on Public Policy* (Vol. 10). Amsterdam: North-Holland.

ZELLNER, A., and PALM, F. (1974) "Time series analysis and simultaneous equation econometric models." *Journal of Econometrics* 2: 17-54.

ABOUT THE AUTHORS

JEFF B. CROMWELL is a Lecturer in the Institute for Labor Studies and a Ph.D. candidate in the Natural Resource Economics program in the College of Agriculture and Forestry at West Virginia University. His research interests have been in the areas of nonlinear time series analysis and resource modeling. His teaching experience includes West Virginia University, Edinboro University of Pennsylvania, California University of Pennsylvania, and the Inter-University Consortium for Political and Social Science Research at the University of Michigan. He has recently published an article on multivariate time series methodology in the *International Regional Science Review.*

MICHAEL J. HANNAN is an Associate Professor of Economics in the Department of Business Administration and Economics at Edinboro University of Pennsylvania. He earned a Ph.D. in Mineral Resource Economics from West Virginia University, where he was also a Senior Research Assistant at the Regional Research Institute. His research interests include economic forecasting, and econometric and input-output modeling. He has published articles on various topics in the *International Regional Science Review, Professional Geographer, Technological Forecasting and Social Change,* and the *Pennsylvania Economic Review.*

WALTER C. LABYS is a Benedum Distinguished Scholar and Professor of Resource Economics at West Virginia University. He is also a Visiting Professor at the Center for Industrial Econometrics at the University of Montpellier, where he collaborated with Michel Terraza on the present text. His interest in time series analysis began before 1970 when he copublished his dissertation, *Speculation, Hedging and Commodity Price Forecasts.* Since then he has published articles on the application of time series methods to international commodity markets in journals such as the *Oxford Bulletin of Economics and Statistics, Applied Economics, Journal of Futures Markets, Journal of Development Studies, Resources Policy, Journal of Policy Modeling, Energy Economics,* and *Weltwirtschaftliches Archives.* He is currently involved with the time series analysis of international commodity markets, inventories, and prices.

MICHEL TERRAZA is a Senior Lecturer in the Faculty of Economics at the University of Montpellier I. He is founder of the Centre d'Econometrie Pour l'Enterprise (C.E.P.E.; the Center for Industrial Econometrics) at the University of Montpellier I. He is also involved with the Research Group on Statistics and Mathematics at the Ecole d'Ingenieurs des Mines d'Ales. His research interests have been in time series analysis, particularly spectral analysis, and univariate and multivariate analysis with a number of industries. His teaching interests include the development of undergraduate, graduate, and short courses on time series analysis. The latter courses have been taught at the management and public policy level. In addition to serving as editor for the C.E.P.E. Working Paper Series, he has also consulted with business and governments on economic conditions and industry development.